Salvador Dalí

The Persistence of Memory

ANNE UMLAND

THE MUSEUM OF MODERN ART, NEW YORK

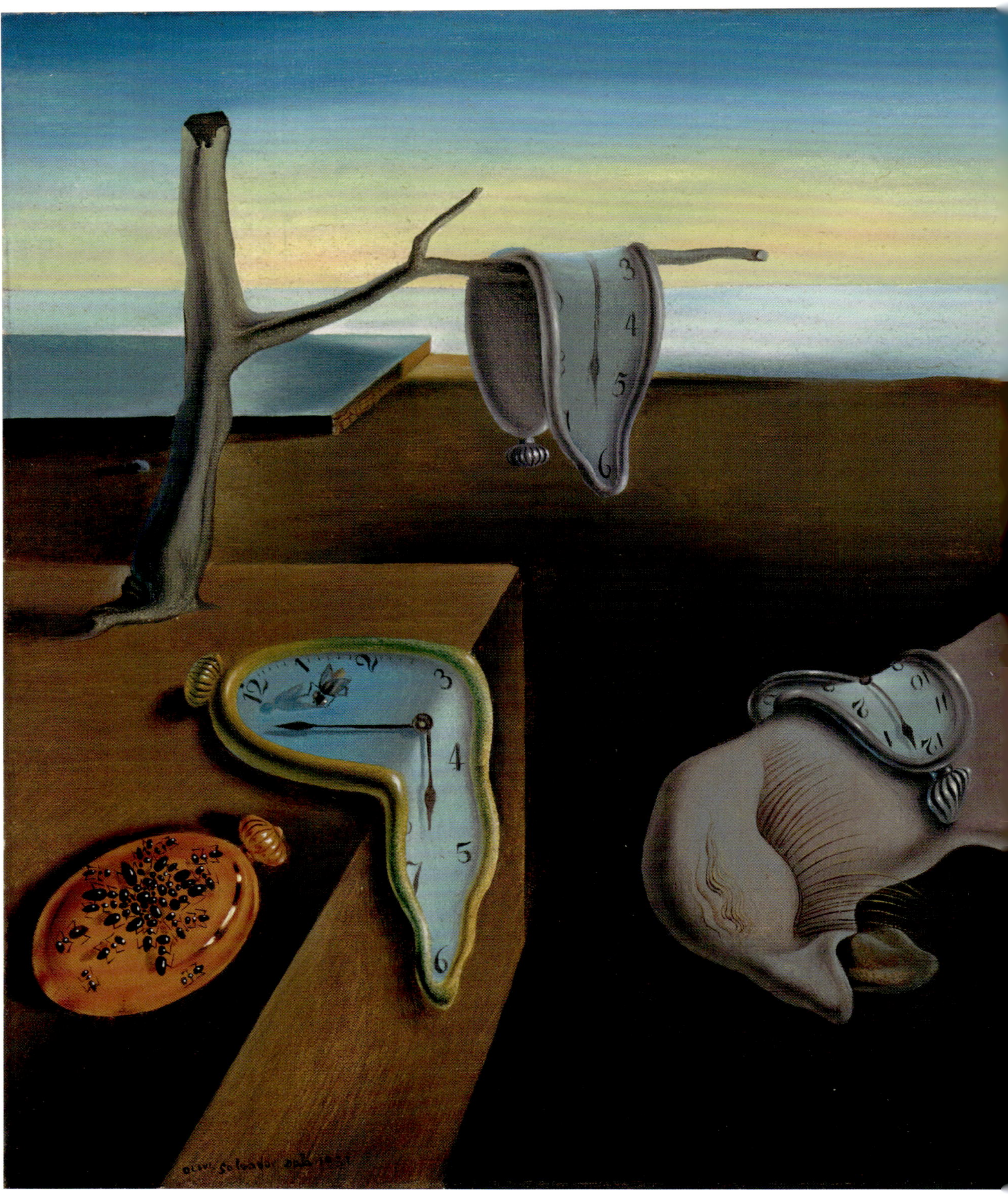

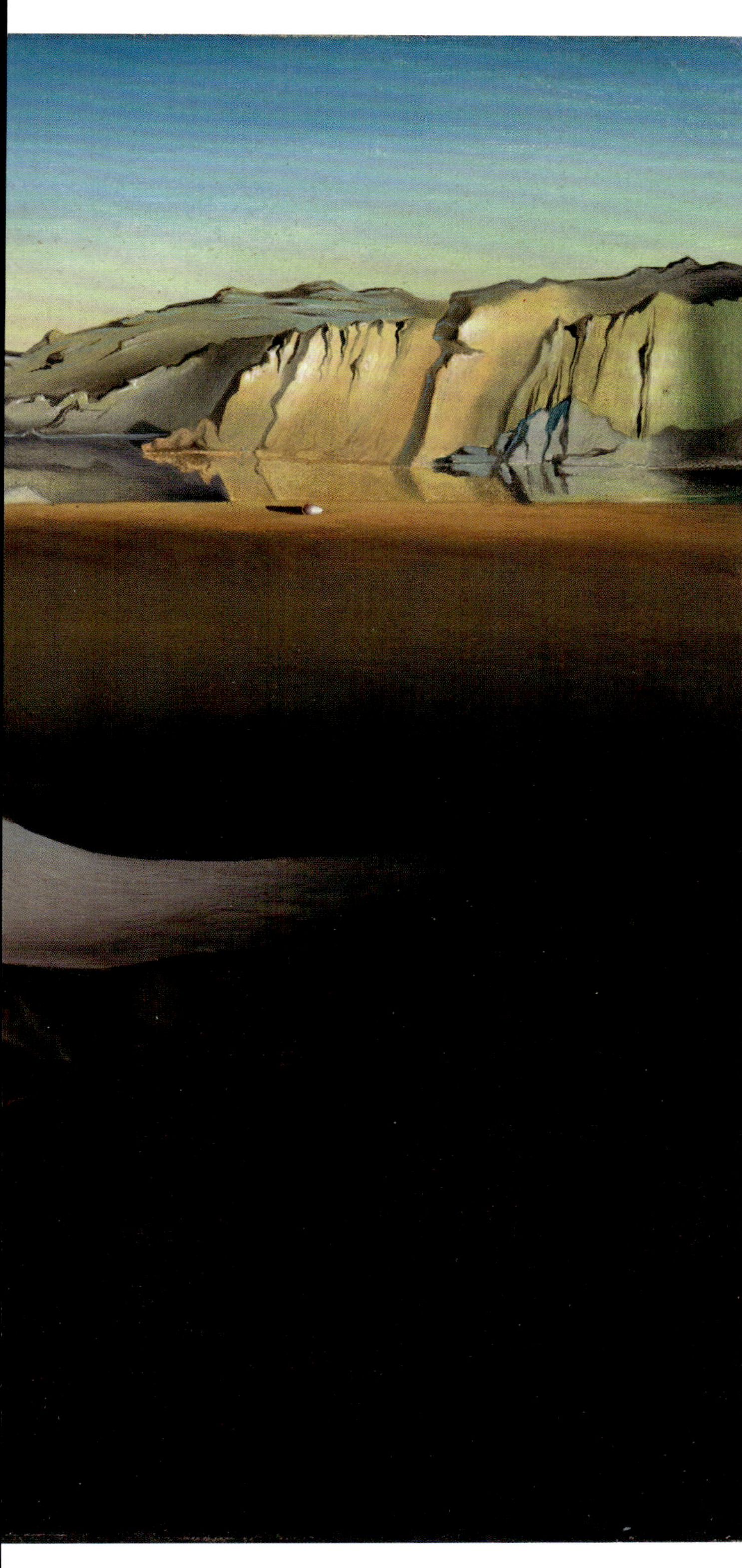

Salvador Dalí (Spanish, 1904–1989). *The Persistence of Memory*. 1931. Oil on canvas, 9 ½ × 13" (24.1 × 33 cm).
THE MUSEUM OF MODERN ART, NEW YORK. GIVEN ANONYMOUSLY

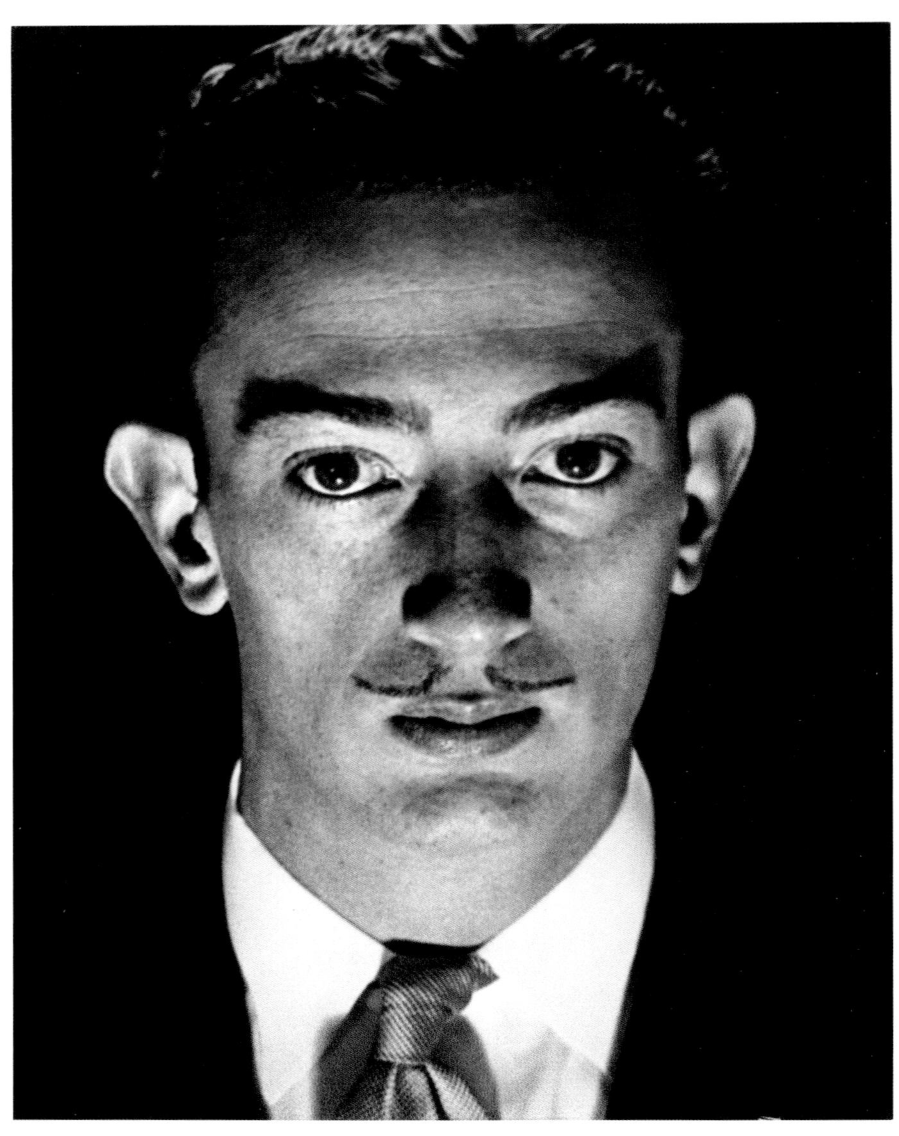

FIG. 1. Man Ray (American, 1890–1976). *Salvador Dalí*. 1929. Gelatin silver print, 9 × 7 1⁄16" (22.9 × 17.9 cm).
THE MUSEUM OF MODERN ART, NEW YORK. GIFT OF JAMES THRALL SOBY

ACCORDING TO SALVADOR DALÍ [FIG. 1], *THE PERSISTENCE OF MEMORY*, HIS FAMOUS Surrealist painting of melting watches, was inspired by a piece of smelly, oozing cheese. "We had topped off our meal with a very strong Camembert," he recalled in *The Secret Life of Salvador Dalí*, his self-mythologizing autobiography, some ten years after he completed his small but unforgettable picture. "And after everyone had gone I remained for a long time seated at the table meditating on the philosophic problems of the 'super-soft' which the cheese presented to my mind."[1] The hour was around ten o'clock at night; the setting, an apartment in Paris at 7, rue Becquerel, a residential street just north of Sacré Coeur in Montmartre, a legendary artists' neighborhood.[2] Having finished contemplating the Camembert, Dalí set to work:

> I got up and went into my studio, where I lit the light in order to cast a final glance, as is my habit, at the picture I was in the midst of painting. This picture represented a landscape near Port Lligat, whose rocks were lighted by a transparent and melancholy twilight; in the foreground an olive tree with its branches cut, and without leaves. I knew that the atmosphere which I had succeeded in creating with this landscape was to serve as a setting for some idea, for some surprising image, but I did not in the least know what it was going to be.[3]

Dalí proceeds to describe a spark of inspiration. "I was about to turn out the light," he wrote, when "instantaneously I 'saw' the solution. I saw two soft watches, one of them hanging lamentably on the branch of the olive tree. . . . I avidly prepared my palette and set to work. . . . Two hours later the picture, which was to be one of my most famous, was completed."[4]

In Dalí's account of his pocket watch–filled picture's creation, time is of the essence. The painting itself, however, tells a different story. A close examination by conservators and conservation scientists at The Museum of Modern Art almost a hundred years after its completion reveals Dalí's chronology to be a malleable narrative, undone at every turn by material and technical analysis. For example, while Dalí makes a point of mentioning the swiftness with which the "surprising image" appeared and the speed with which he executed it, the timeline of two hours is improbable, given the watches' exceptionally detailed rendering and the time required for even thin layers of oil paint to dry. Equally unlikely is Dalí's claim that the barren tree at left was present in its entirety prior to the addition of the watch hanging over its single, outstretched limb. Simply shining a light through the canvas from back to front quickly reveals that this painted branch does not extend beneath the "soft" timepiece, as it would have had the whole tree been painted first. The same holds true for the supports of the two other limp watches featured in the picture. One of them, at lower left, takes the form of a rectangular plinth over which a gold-rimmed watch is draped like a piece of fabric. The other, at lower center, is a quasi-human creature whose features approximate those of Dalí's own face in profile, saddled by a drooping, silver-rimmed watch. Neither plinth nor creature literally extends beneath these watches, as might be expected from Dalí's verbal description and from the pure painterly illusionism of the work itself. Instead, as confirmed by X-ray fluorescence (XRF) scanning **[FIG. 2]**, the artist knew in advance where the primary protagonists of his composition—the three soft watches, an additional solid-seeming one covered with ants, and the Dalinian profile—would be placed within the landscape and in relation to each other, and he therefore left certain areas blank to fill in later.[5]

To point this out in no way diminishes the evocativeness of Dalí's narrative. It does, however, highlight his text's "meaningful falsification of memory," to quote the Surrealist poet André Breton.[6] Dalí wrote *The Secret Life of Salvador Dalí* in 1940–41, a decade after *The Persistence of Memory* was made, at a point when the painting was already famous, resided in MoMA's collection, and had become virtually synonymous with Dalí-the-man and with his art. By portraying it as the pure, unpremeditated result of an unbidden spark of inspiration, provoked by a cheesy chance encounter and featuring a "surprising image" that was set down quickly, before conscious thought could intervene, Dalí reinforced his best-known work's status as an emblem of Surrealism and of his own "paranoiac-critical"[7] method, which allowed him to see—and to paint—ordinarily invisible "associations and facts," like those between a timekeeping device, his own face, and a piece of melting cheese.[8] He also underscored, in a playful, funny, even surreal way, *The Persistence of Memory*'s essential subject: What better way to tell the origin story of a painting that is all about time, both literally and figuratively, than by foregrounding the timeline of its making and how long it took to finish? The work remains to this day one of modern art's most recognizable and widely reproduced images, and Dalí, for many, is known as the artist of the melting watch.

Who was Salvador Dalí? How did he come to be working in an apartment-cum-studio in Paris in 1931, the year *The Persistence of Memory* was completed? Although today he is one of the twentieth century's best-known artists, famous for his hallucinatory, minutely detailed images and his outlandish persona—the latter a work of

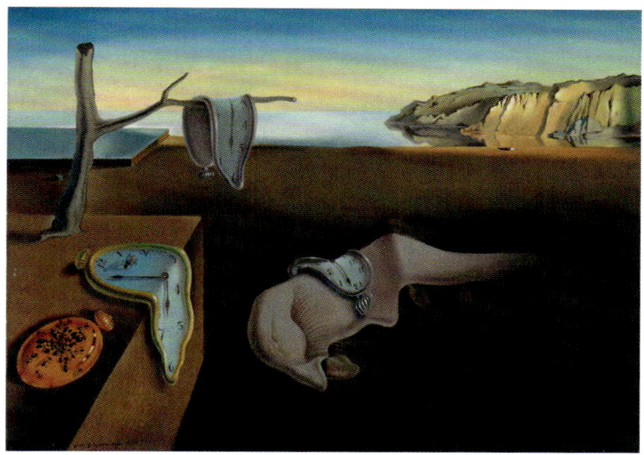
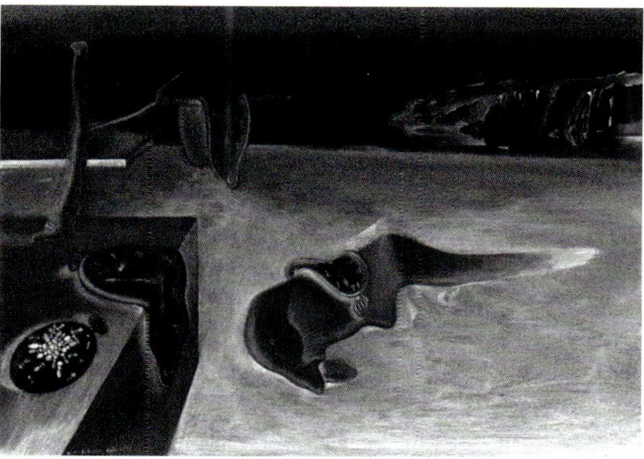
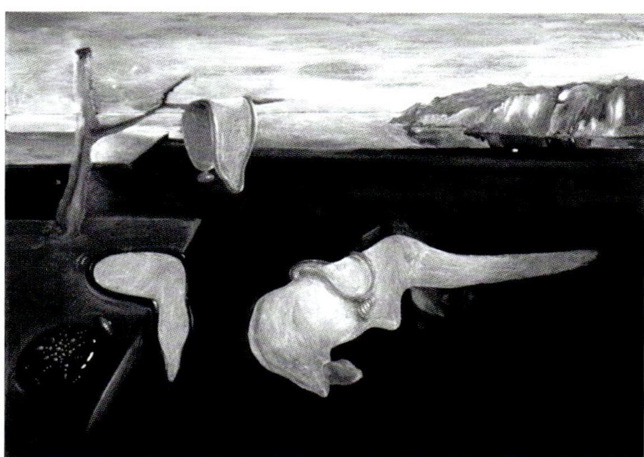
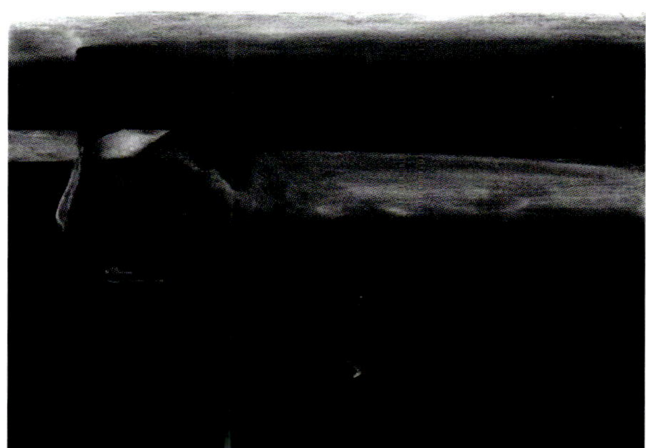
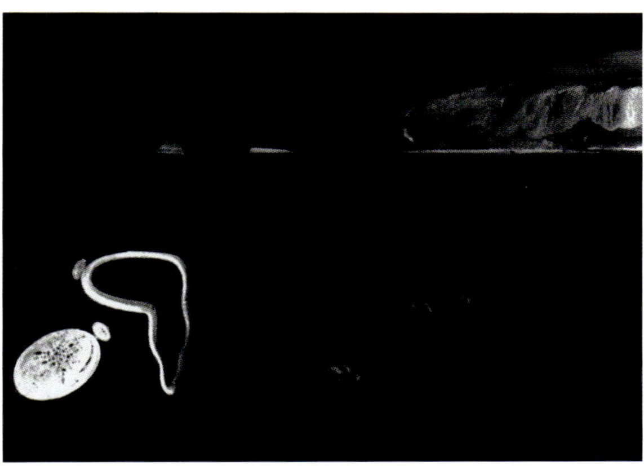
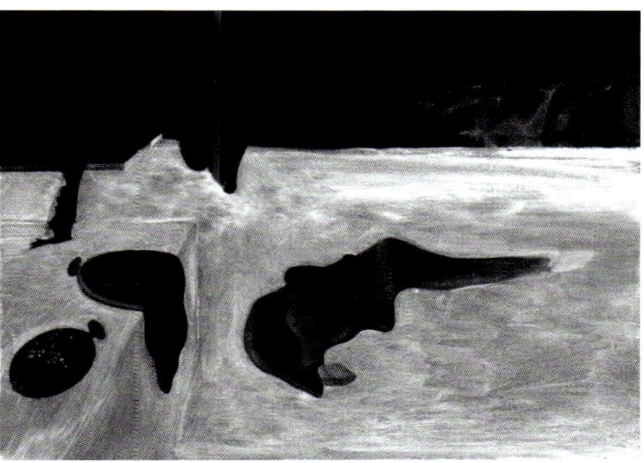

FIG. 2. X-ray fluorescence (XRF) maps identifying the location of specific pigments. Left to right, top to bottom: *The Persistence of Memory*, bone black, zinc white, cerulean blue, chrome yellow/orange, earth brown. The sharp contours of each element indicate that many of them were accounted for early in the composition, and that the artist likely completed the painting over a period of weeks—not overnight

art in and of itself—in 1931, he was only twenty-seven and at the very beginning of his meteoric rise to international renown. Born in 1904 in Figueres, a small Catalan city near the French border in northeastern Spain, Dalí was raised in a prosperous upper-middle-class family. His mother, whom he loved dearly, died in 1921, when he was only seventeen. His father, a distinguished notary, was initially supportive of his precociously talented son's desire to become an artist. He financed Dalí's studies at Madrid's prestigious Real Academia de Bellas Artes de San Fernando, which offered "instruction in the formal discipline of oil painting and academic art," up until Dalí's expulsion in 1926 for having declared, during his examinations, that none of his professors were competent to judge him.[9] Dalí's father was also the subject of several early portraits, including *Portrait of My Father* **[FIG. 3]**, rendered in a quasi-Symbolist style, in which Dalí portrayed him sporting an old-fashioned pocket watch suspended from a chain stretched across his ample belly; the reappearance of this paternal attribute —limp and nonfunctional—in *The Persistence of Memory* suggests a Freudian resonance the artist would certainly have been familiar with.[10] That Dalí senior remained a keen observer of his son's career through the late 1920s is evidenced by a May 17, 1929, letter to the artist Joan Miró, an early advocate for his younger Catalan compatriot's work, in which he thanked Miró for his important role in helping his son secure his first contract with the Paris dealer Camille Goemans.[11] By the end of that same pivotal year, however—during which Dalí shifted the center of his activities from the circles of the Catalan avant-garde to those of the Paris Surrealists and created a spectacular new series of psychoanalytically inflected, hallucinatory, and hyperreal paintings—he and his father had become acrimoniously estranged.

Dalí had arrived in the French capital in late March or early April 1929 to work with the filmmaker Luis Buñuel, whom he knew from his student days in Madrid, on the soon-to-become notorious film *Un Chien andalou*. He was also acting on Miró's advice that he come to Paris for a few months, to "[prepare] the ground *yourself*" for an eventual exhibition. "I have friends here who think highly of you," Miró told him, "all of whom would do everything they can to give us ammunition"; he then went on to warn, "If you don't do this, it's almost certain to pass virtually unnoticed, neutralizing your attack and at the same time, removing you from the action for a long time, since an exhibition which is to have a *real sting* needs more than weeks or even months to prepare."[12] Miró's belligerent language was in keeping with Dalí's own, as expressed in correspondence with his close friend the Andalusian poet Federico García Lorca, and in his writing for Catalan publications such as *L'Amic de les Arts*, in which he frequently used terms such as "putrefaction" and "putrefieds" to describe what he considered to be the moribund state of society and the arts in Catalonia.[13] By April 9, 1929, Miró was able to report back home to the Catalan art critic Sebastià Gasch, a mutual friend, that "last night I was with Dalí and we have already started *working*. . . .

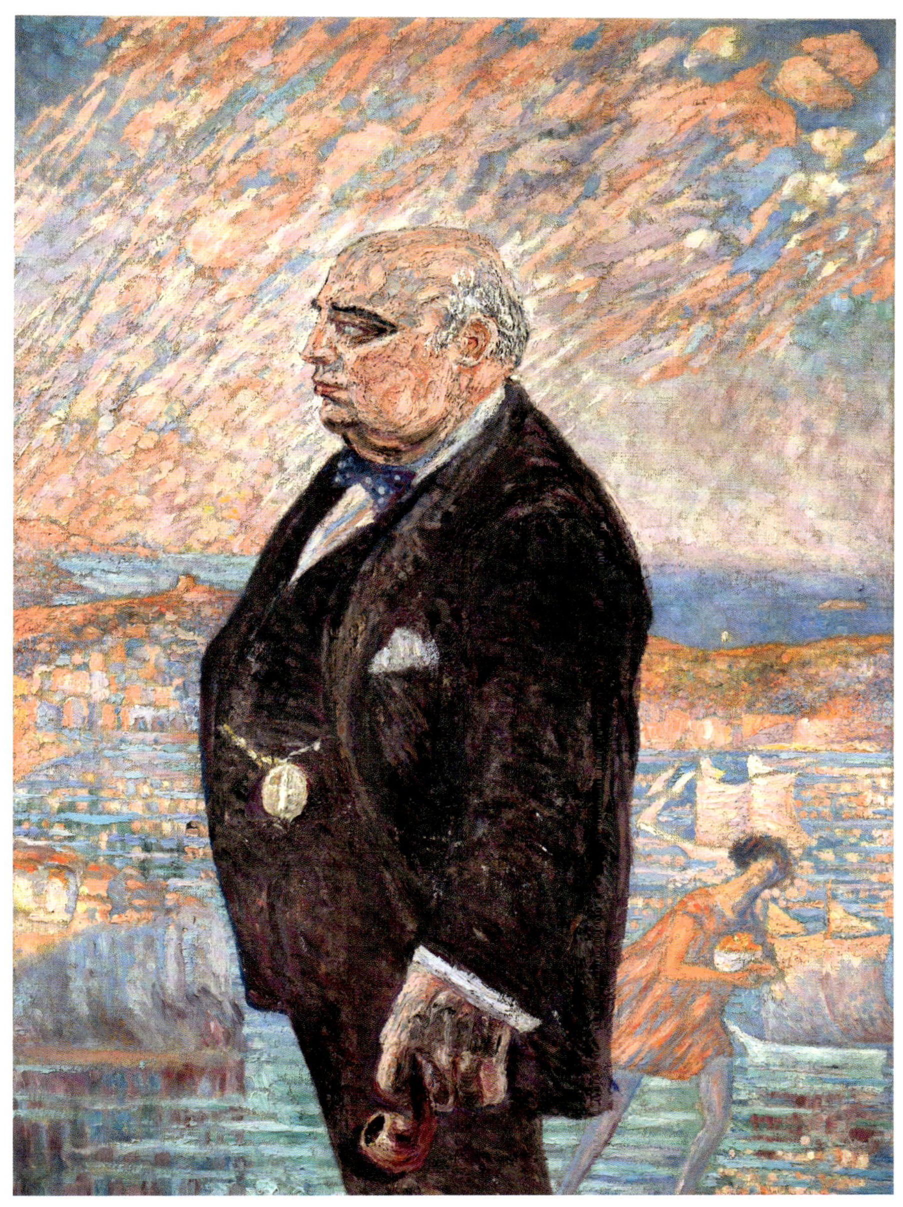

FIG. 3. Salvador Dalí (Spanish, 1904–1989). *Portrait of My Father*. 1920–21. Oil on canvas, 35 13⁄16 × 26 3⁄16" (91 × 66.5 cm). FUNDACIÓ GALA-SALVADOR DALÍ, FIGUERES. DALÍ BEQUEST

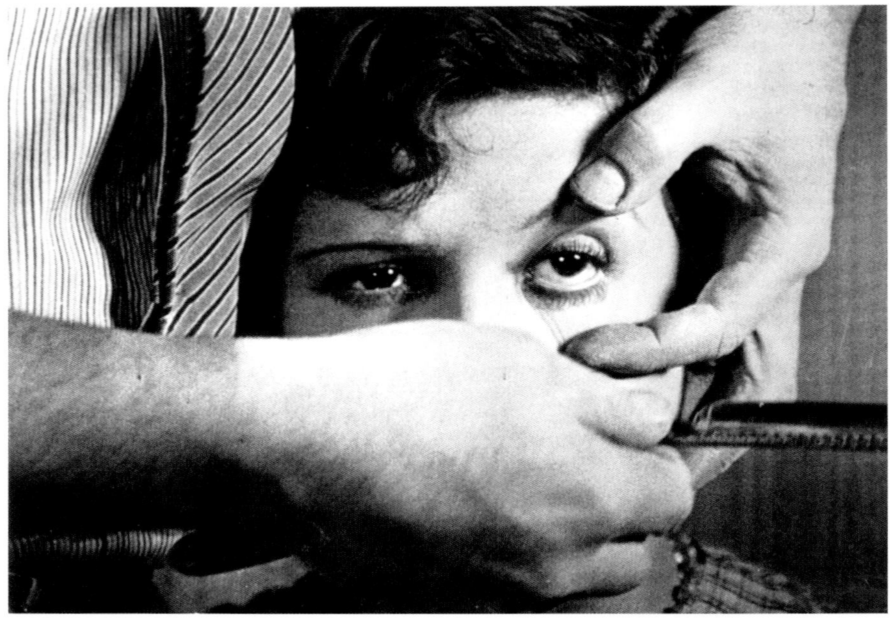

FIG. 4. Luis Buñuel (Spanish, 1900–1983). *Un Chien andalou*. 1929. 35mm film (black and white, silent), approx. 16 min. Produced by Luis Buñuel and Salvador Dalí. THE MUSEUM OF MODERN ART, NEW YORK

I have the strong feeling that Dalí has arrived here at a very good moment, and that he *will make an impact*."[14] Miró's words proved prophetic: On June 6, *Un Chien andalou* previewed at the Studio des Ursulines cinema in Paris. With its shocking montage sequences—including the scandalous opening image of a hand drawing a razor quickly across a wide-open eye [**FIG. 4**]—it was a great success among the Surrealists, many of whom, thanks to Miró's introductions, Dalí now personally knew. Stimulated by Goemans's promises of a contract and a fall exhibition, he returned sometime in June to his family's summer home in Cadaqués, a picturesque town on the Mediterranean's Costa Brava, and began to prepare in earnest for his solo Paris debut.

Of the eleven paintings included in that exhibition, which opened on November 25, 1929, with a catalogue whose preface was authored by Breton, only two were completed prior to that year. One of those was the proto-Surrealist and astonishingly intricate *Futile Efforts (Little Ashes)* [**FIG. 5**], which included the heads of Dalí at left and García Lorca at right.[15] The other nine were recent creations that ranged in size from relatively large oils on canvas, such as the extraordinary pair constituted by *Face of the Great Masturbator* [**FIG. 6**] and *The Enigma of Desire* [**FIG. 7**], to the bordering-on-miniature *Illumined Pleasures* [**FIG. 8**], *The Accommodations of Desire* [**FIG. 9**], and *The Lugubrious Game* [**FIG. 10**], each with fanatically

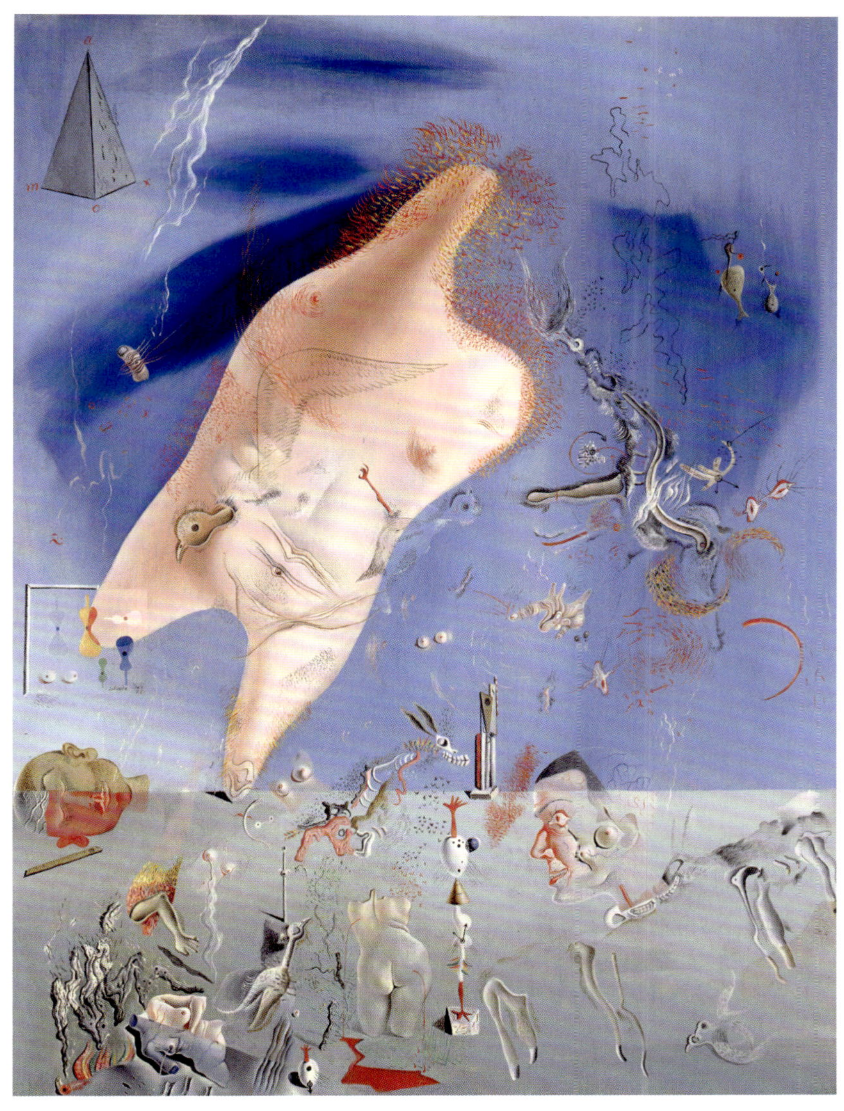

FIG. 5. Salvador Dalí (Spanish, 1904–1989). *Futile Efforts (Little Ashes)*. 1927–28. Oil on plywood panel, 25 3⁄16 × 18 7⁄8" (64 × 48 cm). MUSEO NACIONAL CENTRO DE ARTE REINA SOFÍA, MADRID

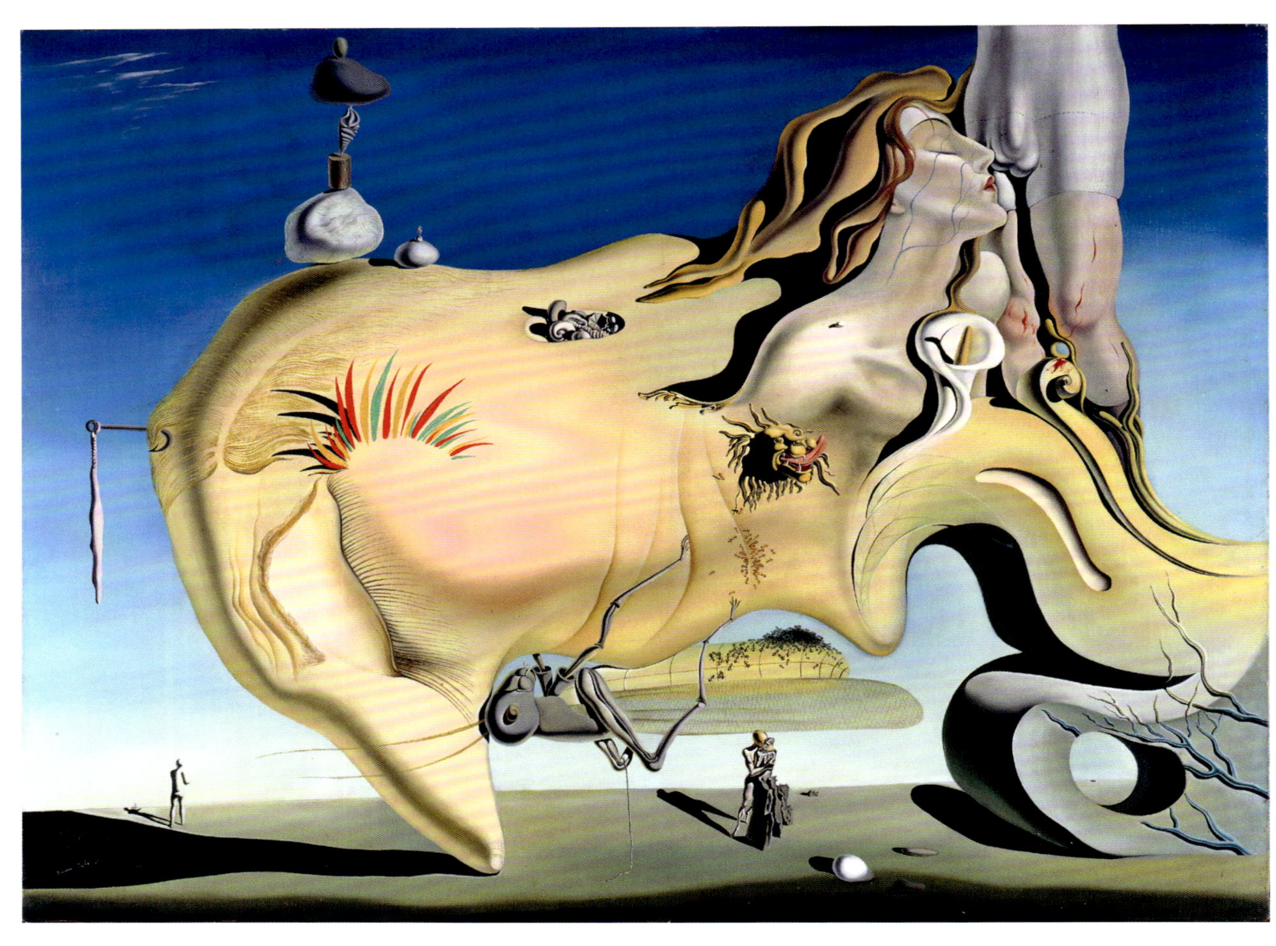

FIG. 6. Salvador Dalí (Spanish, 1904–1989). *Face of the Great Masturbator.* 1929. Oil on canvas, 43 5⁄16 × 59 1⁄16" (110 × 150 cm). MUSEO NACIONAL CENTRO DE ARTE REINA SOFÍA, MADRID. SALVADOR DALÍ BEQUEST

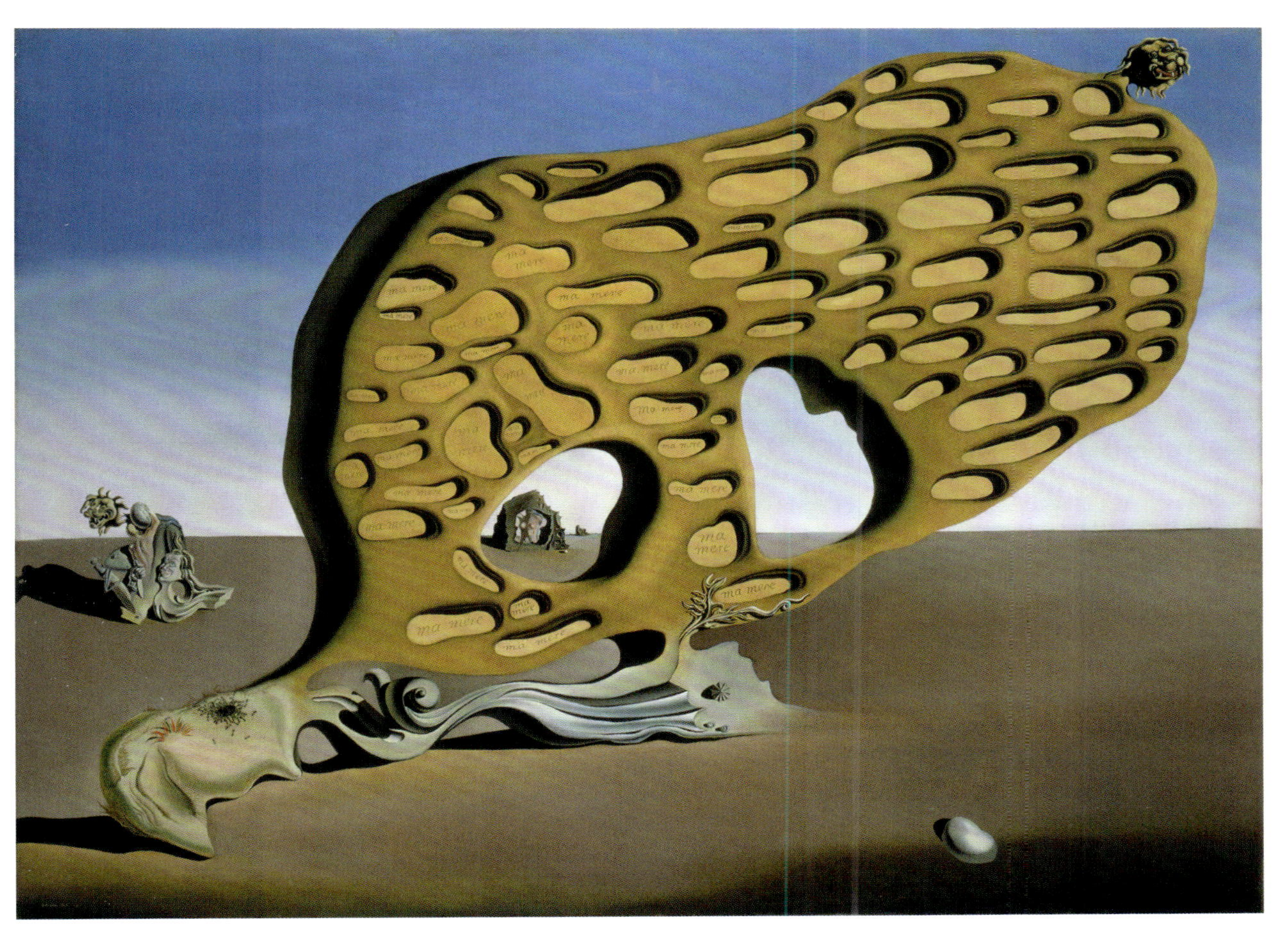

FIG. 7. Salvador Dalí (Spanish, 1904–1989). *The Enigma of Desire*. 1929. Oil on canvas, 43 ½ × 59 ¼" (110.5 × 150.5 cm).
BAYERISCHE STAATSGEMÄLDESAMMLUNGEN, SAMMLUNG MODERNE KUNST, PINAKOTHEK DER MODERNE, MUNICH

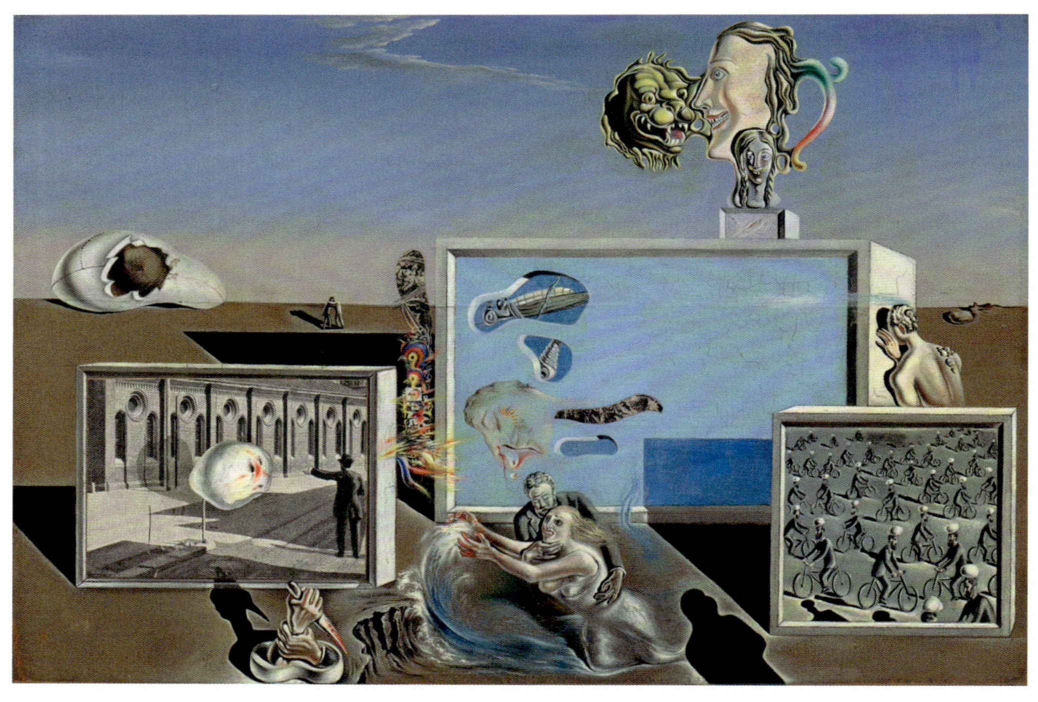

FIG. 8. Salvador Dalí (Spanish, 1904–1989). *Illumined Pleasures.* 1929. Oil and collage on board, 9 ⅜ × 13 ⅝" (23.8 × 34.7 cm). THE MUSEUM OF MODERN ART, NEW YORK. THE SIDNEY AND HARRIET JANIS COLLECTION

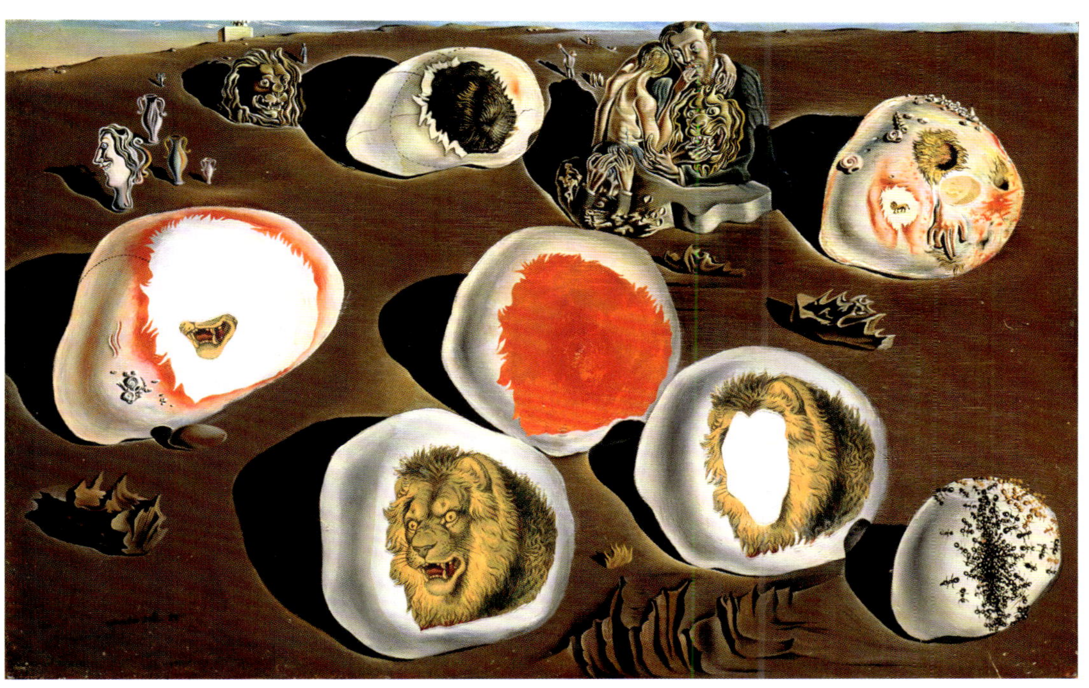

FIG. 9. Salvador Dalí (Spanish, 1904–1989). *The Accommodations of Desire*. 1929. Oil and cut-and-pasted printed paper on wood, 8 ¾ × 13 ¾" (22.2 × 34.9 cm). THE METROPOLITAN MUSEUM OF ART, NEW YORK. JACQUES AND NATASHA GELMAN COLLECTION

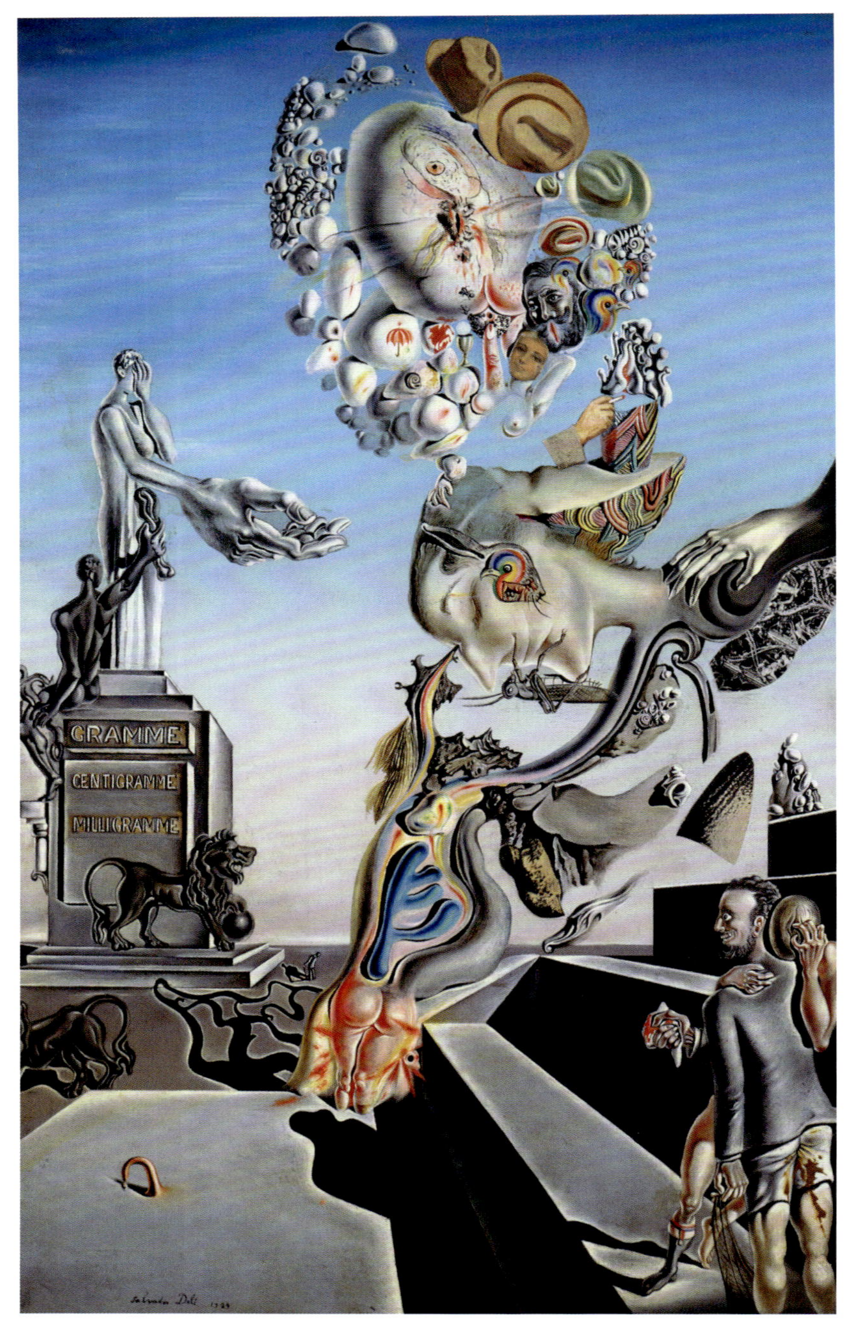

FIG. 10. Salvador Dalí (Spanish, 1904–1989). *The Lugubrious Game*. 1929. Oil and collage on cardboard, 17 ½ × 11 15⁄16" (44.4 × 30.3 cm). PRIVATE COLLECTION

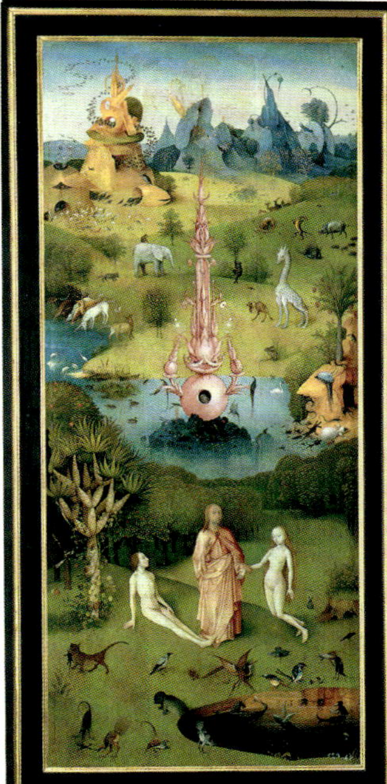
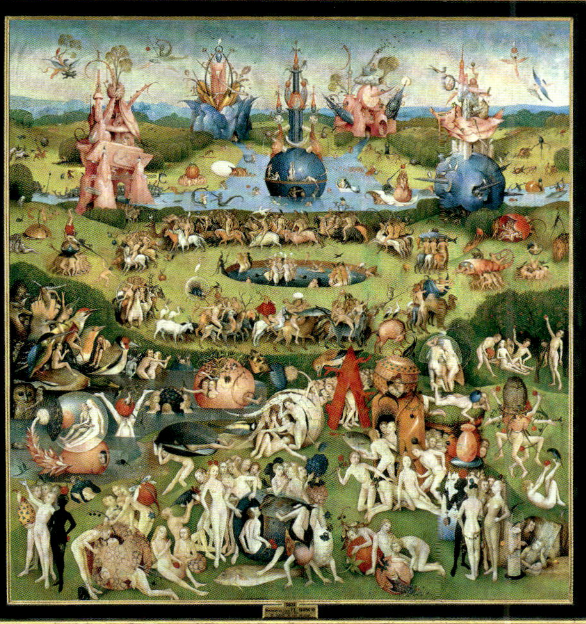
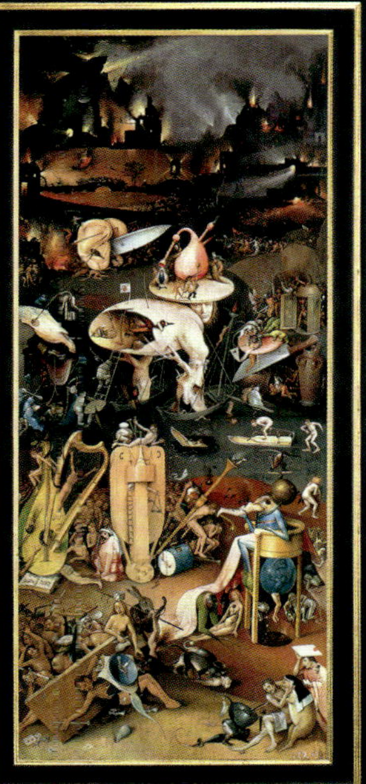

FIG. 11. Hieronymus Bosch (Dutch, c. 1450–1516). *The Garden of Earthly Delights.* 1490–1500. Oil on three oak panels, central panel: 6′ 1 ⅛″ × 67 ⅞″ (185.8 × 172.5 cm); side panels, each: 6′ 1 ⅛″ × 30 ⅛″ (185.8 × 76.5 cm). MUSEO NACIONAL DEL PRADO, MADRID

detailed trompe-l'oeil painted motifs interspersed with collaged readymade images. Collectively, these nine paintings represent a tour de force; they set a new course for Dalí's art in terms of their technical precision, their "dreamlike [settings] in a deep space," and their complex iconography informed by the artist's readings of psychoanalytic texts, notably Richard von Krafft-Ebing's *Psychopathia Sexualis* (1886) and Sigmund Freud's explorations of the subconscious mind.[16] Each picture brought childhood memories and anxieties of a sexual nature to the surface: castration, voyeurism, onanism, and impotence, along with recurrent images of things that inspired Dalí with horror and disgust, including ants, grasshoppers, blood, and excrement. Moreover, as Miró had predicted, Dalí's new body of work premiered in Paris "at a very good moment," one that found Breton's Surrealist movement at a crossroads, poised between the First and Second Surrealist Manifestoes and ready for a new sensation. Dalí's unsettling and unprecedented paintings, following on his and Buñuel's equally unsettling and unprecedented film, provided just that. They were unlike anything the Surrealists, or anyone for that matter, had seen before, despite qualities shared with works by Old Master fantasists such as Hieronymus Bosch **[FIG. 11]**, and with modern paintings by contemporaries such as Giorgio de Chirico **[FIG. 12]**, Max Ernst **[FIG. 13]**, Miró **[FIG. 14]**, and Yves Tanguy **[FIG. 15]**. A photomontage

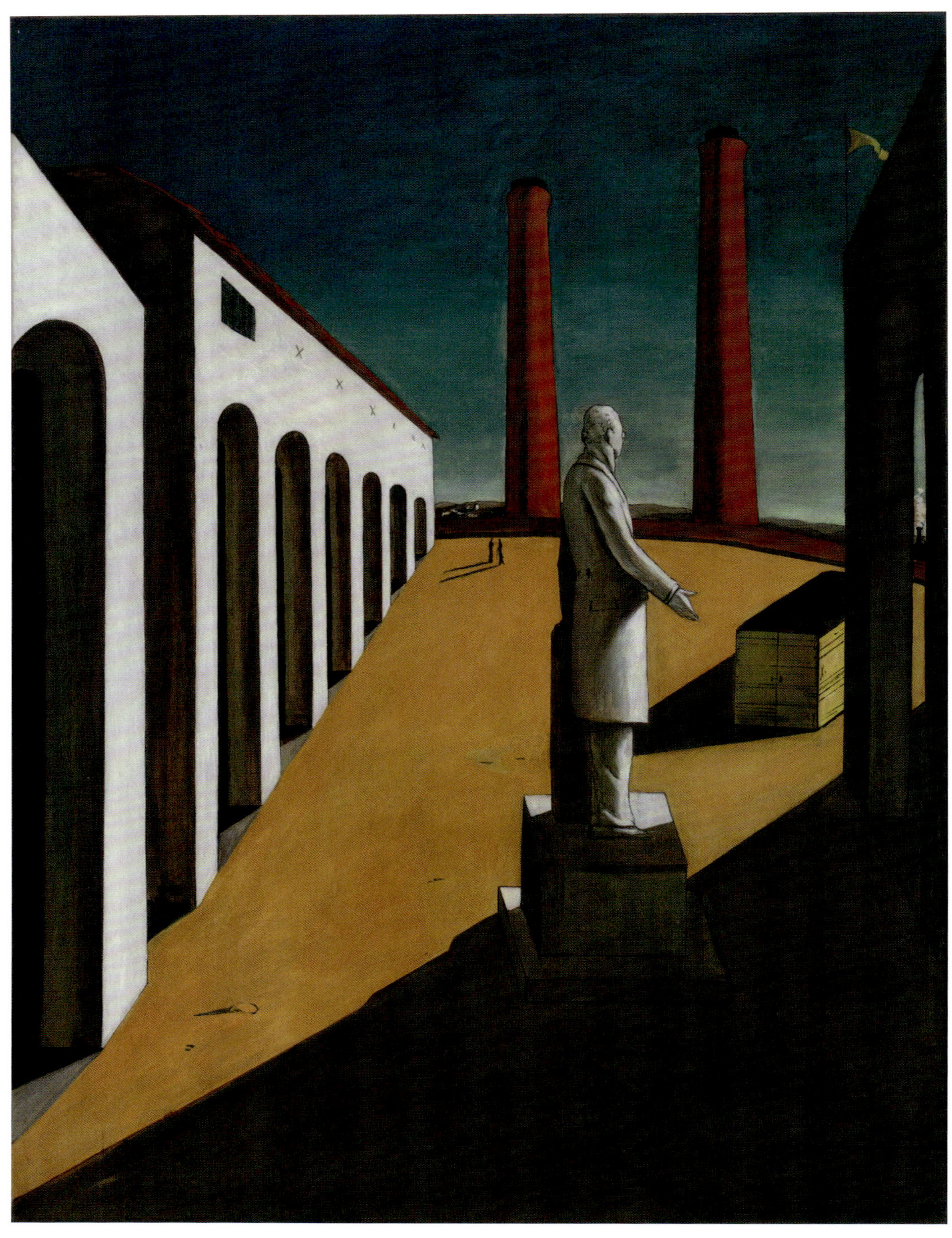

FIG. 12. Giorgio de Chirico (Italian, born Greece. 1888–1978). *The Enigma of a Day*. 1914. Oil on canvas, 6' 1" × 55" (185.5 × 139.7 cm). THE MUSEUM OF MODERN ART, NEW YORK. JAMES THRALL SOBY BEQUEST

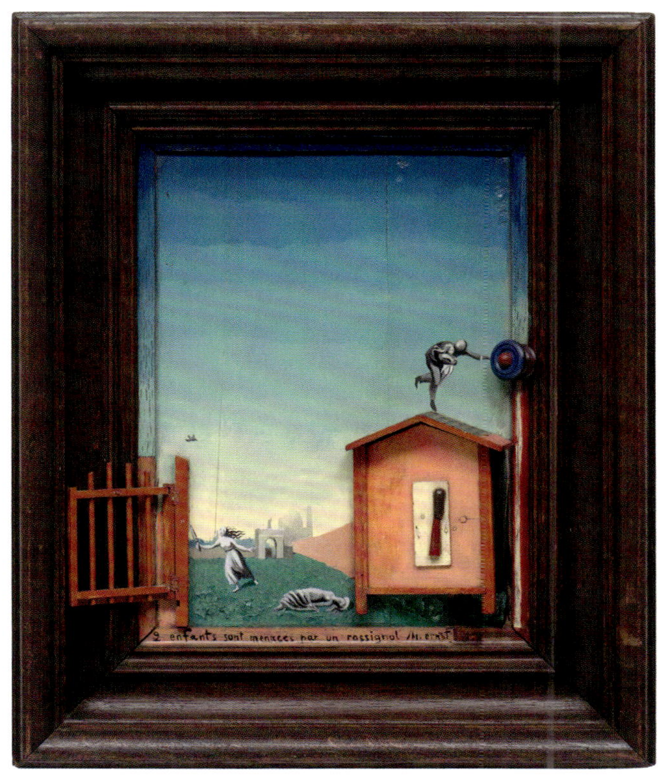

FIG. 13. Max Ernst (French and American, born Germany. 1891–1976). *Two Children Are Threatened by a Nightingale*. 1924. Oil with painted wood elements and cut-and-pasted printed paper on wood with wood frame, 27 ½ × 22 ½ × 4 ½" (69.8 × 57.1 × 11.4 cm). THE MUSEUM OF MODERN ART, NEW YORK. PURCHASE

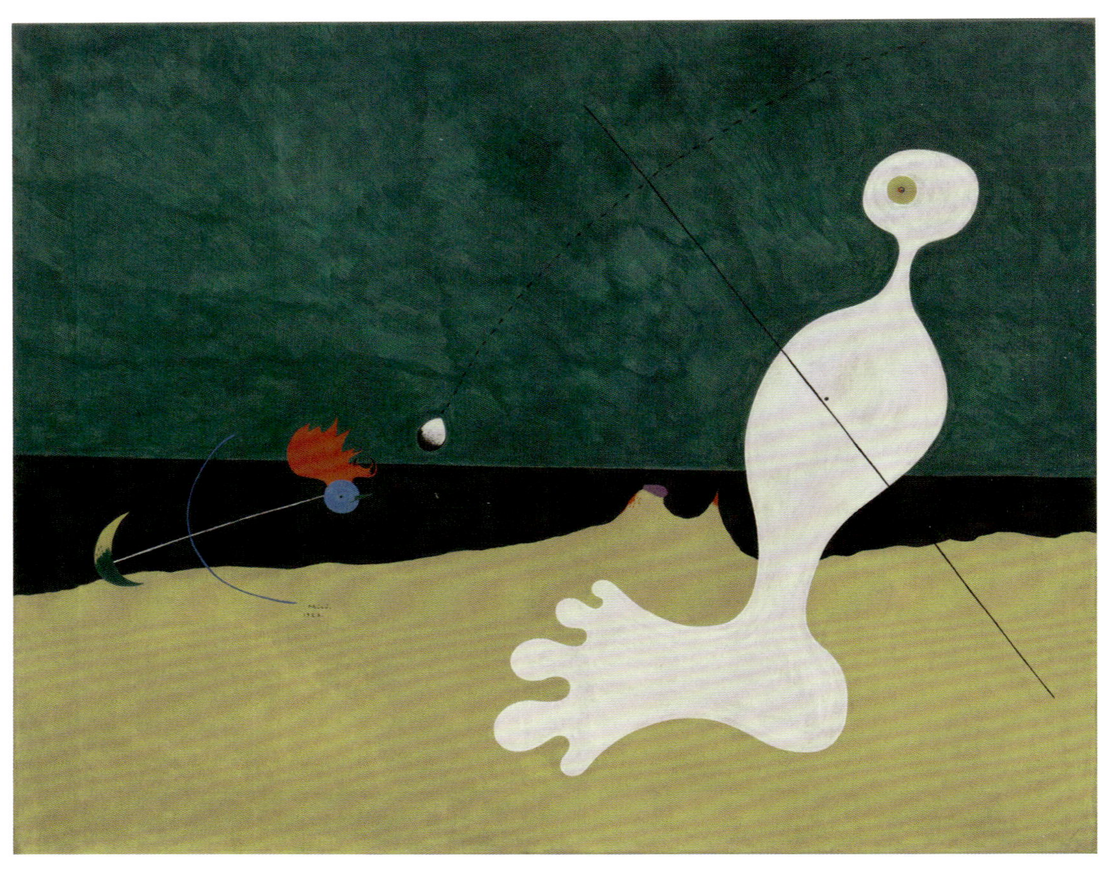

FIG. 14. Joan Miró (Spanish, 1893–1983). *Person Throwing a Stone at a Bird.* 1926. Oil on canvas, 29 × 36 ¼" (73.7 × 92.1 cm). THE MUSEUM OF MODERN ART, NEW YORK. PURCHASE

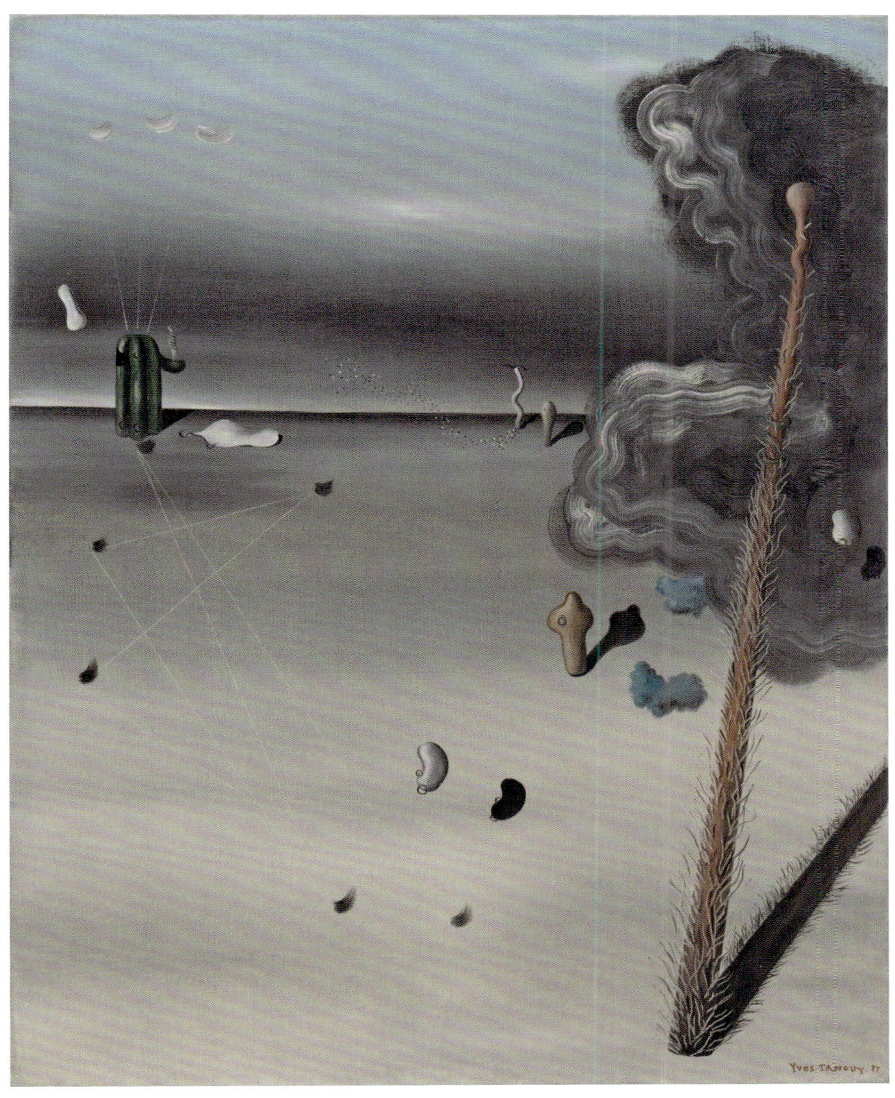

FIG. 15. Yves Tanguy (American, born France. 1900–1955). *Mama, Papa Is Wounded!*. 1927. Oil on canvas, 36 ¼ × 28 ¾" (92.1 × 73 cm). THE MUSEUM OF MODERN ART, NEW YORK. PURCHASE

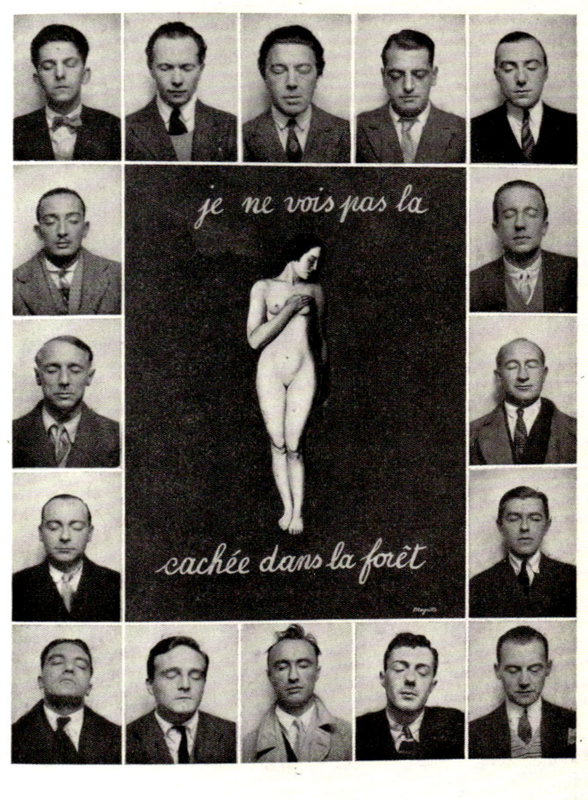

FIG. 16. Portraits of sixteen Surrealists surrounding a reproduction of René Magritte's *The Hidden Woman* (1929), in *La Révolution surréaliste*, no. 12 (December 15, 1929). Dalí is second from the top in the left-hand column.

published in the final issue of *La Révolution surréaliste*, in December 1929, marks his acceptance into the Paris Surrealist group **[FIG. 16]**. In it, Dalí's portrait appeared with those of fifteen other Surrealists, all with eyes closed, a sign of solidarity and of their collective renunciation of the external world in favor of the psyche's inner realm. Two of Dalí's new paintings, *Illumined Pleasures* and *The Accommodations of Desire*, purchased from the Goemans exhibition by the Surrealist poet Louis Aragon and by Breton, respectively, along with the scenario for *Un Chien andalou*, were reproduced in that same issue, confirming Dalí's association with the group.

The end of 1929 also found Dalí deeply and madly in love with the married older woman who was to become his lifelong partner: the Russian-born Gala Éluard **[FIG. 17]**, whom he had met in the summer of 1929 when she had paid Dalí a visit in Cadaqués with a group made up of her then husband, the Surrealist

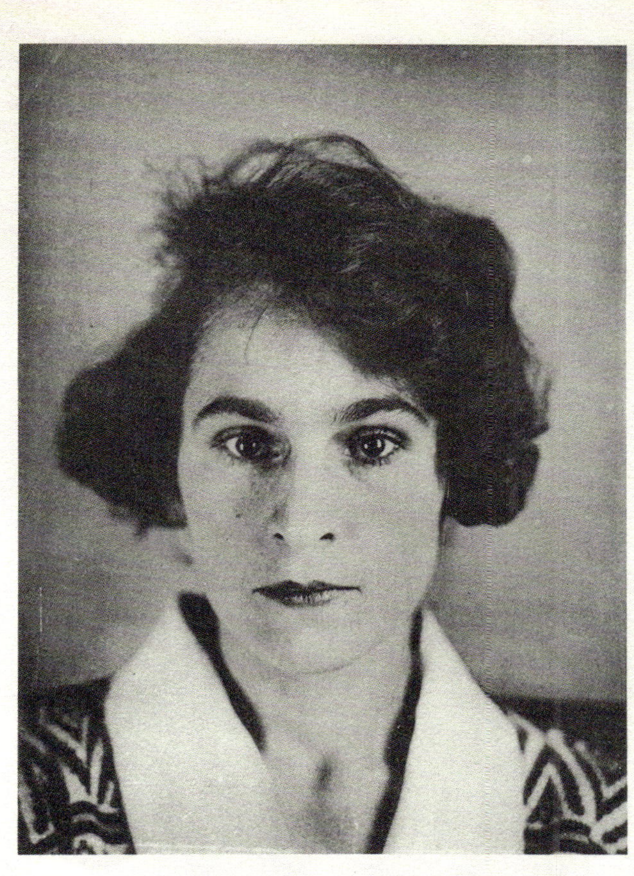

GALA

FIG. 17. Man Ray (American, 1890–1976). *Portrait of Gala* from Salvador Dalí, *The Visible Woman*. 1930. Photogravure from an illustrated book with eight photogravures (one with engraving), plate: 6 15⁄16 × 5 1⁄16" (17.6 × 12.9 cm); page, each: 11 1⁄8 × 8 1⁄4" (28.2 × 21 cm). Publisher: Éditions surréalistes, Paris. Printer: Lacourière, Paris. THE MUSEUM OF MODERN ART, NEW YORK. GIFT OF WALTER CHRYSLER

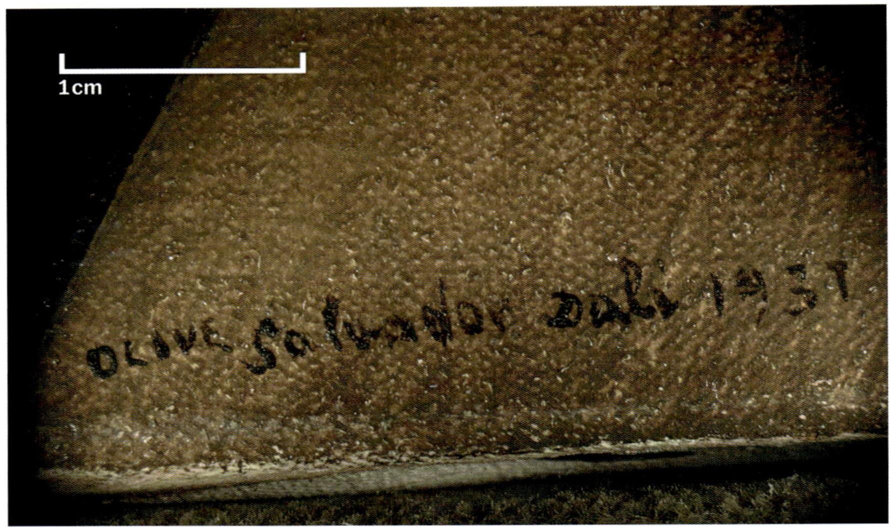

FIG. 18. *The Persistence of Memory,* detail photographed at 6x magnification

poet Paul Éluard; Buñuel; the artist René Magritte and his wife, Georgette; and Goemans and his companion, Yvonne Bernard. Dalí missed the opening of his own exhibition at Galerie Goemans in late November 1929 because he had left two days earlier with Gala for Barcelona and Sitges. Several months later, back in Paris in spring 1930, the couple moved into the rue Becquerel apartment, which had been rented by Paul Éluard. That same year, Dalí began to acknowledge Gala's important role in his work's development by signing his paintings with both of their names. *The Persistence of Memory* is one such painting. Clearly visible in its lower-left corner is the inscription "Olive Salvador Dalí 1931" **[FIG. 18]**. "Olive" was one of his many nicknames for Gala: "I call my wife: Gala, Galuchka, Gradiva (because she has been my Gradiva), Olive (because of the oval of her face and the color of her skin)."[17] Gala was, Dalí notes in *The Secret Life*, the very first person—other than the artist himself—to set eyes on *The Persistence of Memory* once finished. "I made her sit down in front of it with her eyes shut,"[18] Dalí tells us, and then,

> "One, two, three, open your eyes!" I looked intently at Gala's face, and I saw upon it the unmistakable contraction of wonder and astonishment. This convinced me of the effectiveness of my new image, for Gala never errs in judging the authenticity of an enigma. I asked her, "Do you think that in three years you will have forgotten this image?" [Gala replied,] "No one can forget it once he has seen it."

Dalí's writing of Gala into his painting's creation myth makes clear that his signing of her name to *The Persistence of Memory* was no empty romantic gesture; rather, it recognized her agency and power as his coconspirator and as the first viewer, experiencer, and judge of his enigmatic new work.

Dalí most likely made *The Persistence of Memory* between January and May 1931, in the months immediately prior to his second one-person Paris exhibition, this time at Galerie Pierre Colle. Measuring a mere 9½ by 13 inches (24.1 by 33 cm), the work is part landscape, part still life, and part unconventional vanitas. It is painted in oil on a prestretched and preprimed canvas and suffused with the crystalline light and meticulous details that are hallmarks of miniature painting—a small-format tradition, dating back to early sixteenth-century Europe, well suited to Dalí's obsession with miniscule detail and tiny subjects such as ants, flies, and filament-thin hairs.[19] Despite Dalí's penchant for hyperbole, his description of Gala's reaction to it accurately captures the indelible character of the painting and of the sagging watches within it. Once seen, whether in person or in reproduction, they truly are unforgettable. This is due, at least in part, to the intrinsic familiarity of the watches. Although by the time *The Persistence of Memory* was painted, pocket watches were already anachronistic and infrequently used, the mind instantly registers their malleable state as an aberration, as an illogical, irrational deviation from how they are known to be. All the better, as Dalí wrote in 1930, to "systematize confusion and thereby contribute to a total discrediting of the world of reality."[20] The watches' locations and relative size also contribute to their disturbing effect: Instead of hanging from a watch chain or resting on a dresser or tucked away in a drawer, they loom preternaturally large in the immediate foreground of a hauntingly empty and strangely still landscape. Although the exquisitely detailed, irregularly surfaced cliffs at upper right do resemble, as Dalí said, those of the landscape near Port Lligat, on the coast of Catalonia, where he had recently purchased a fisherman's cottage, various elements in the painting quickly establish that it is a dreamscape rather than a real-life scene: the disorienting relationship between things that are very near and those that are very far away; the interplay of golden light and ominous shadow; and the contrasts between natural rock formations, hard-edged geometric platforms, and soft things—not just the three watches but also the fleshy creature in the foreground. So, too, does the closed (as opposed to open) pocket watch at lower left, which is covered by a swarm of ants that eerily converges on its center, creating a creepy-crawly yet jewellike pattern. Their presence implies that this watch, like its less-solid counterparts, is subject to entropy and the forces of nature, has a soft bodily center, can be eaten away at, and inevitably will degrade over time, in keeping with Dalí's obsessional themes of death, decay, and eroticism.

What no reproduction can possibly capture is the small painting's mysterious luminosity, nor the intense delicacy and precision of its details—the cerulean blue

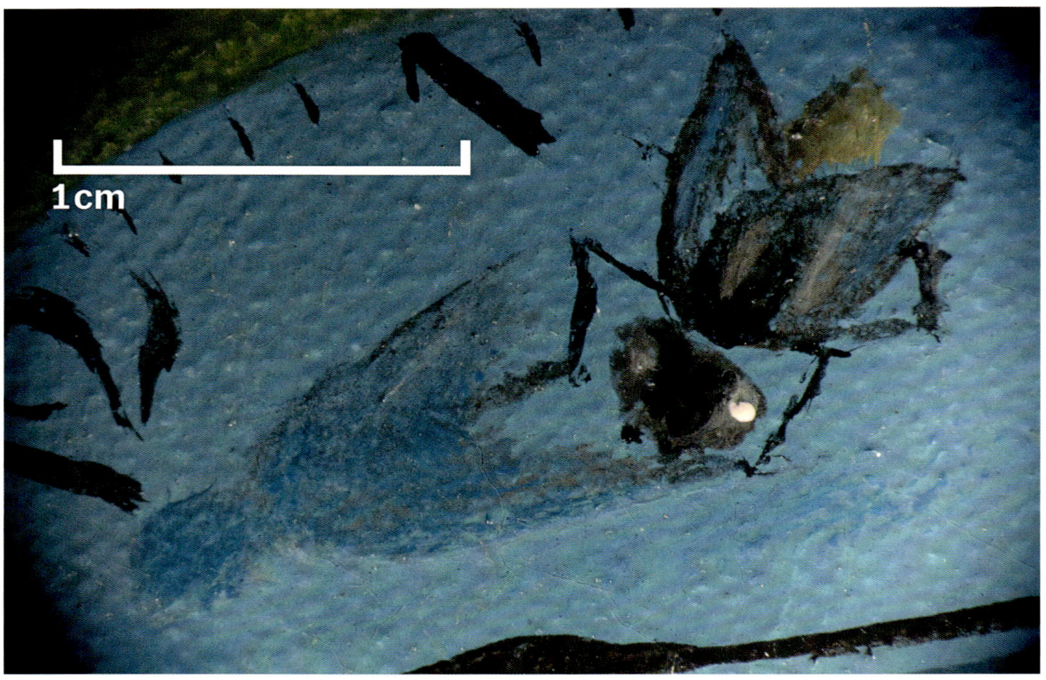

FIG. 19. *The Persistence of Memory,* detail photographed at 10x magnification

shadow beneath the fly [**FIG. 19**], for example, or the zinc-white highlights on the ants [**FIG. 20**]—and even those are best appreciated with the aid of a microscope, just as Dalí most likely painted them using some form of magnifying device and very tiny brushes. Scientific imaging further reveals how he used broader strokes of earth brown to paint the pedestal where the watches lie, added chrome yellow and orange to gild them, and enhanced his ants' glittering, gemlike character by using daubs of zinc white beneath bone-black paint like a modeling element, to build dimension before applying final touches of zinc white for highlights [**FIG. 21**]. He also used zinc white to render the flaccid foreground figure. Its left side appears three-dimensional due to Dalí's skillful modeling and shading. On the right, however, it flattens out and seems to dissolve into nothingness; Dalí produced this effect by painting over the tip of its trailing neck-cum-tail with the same

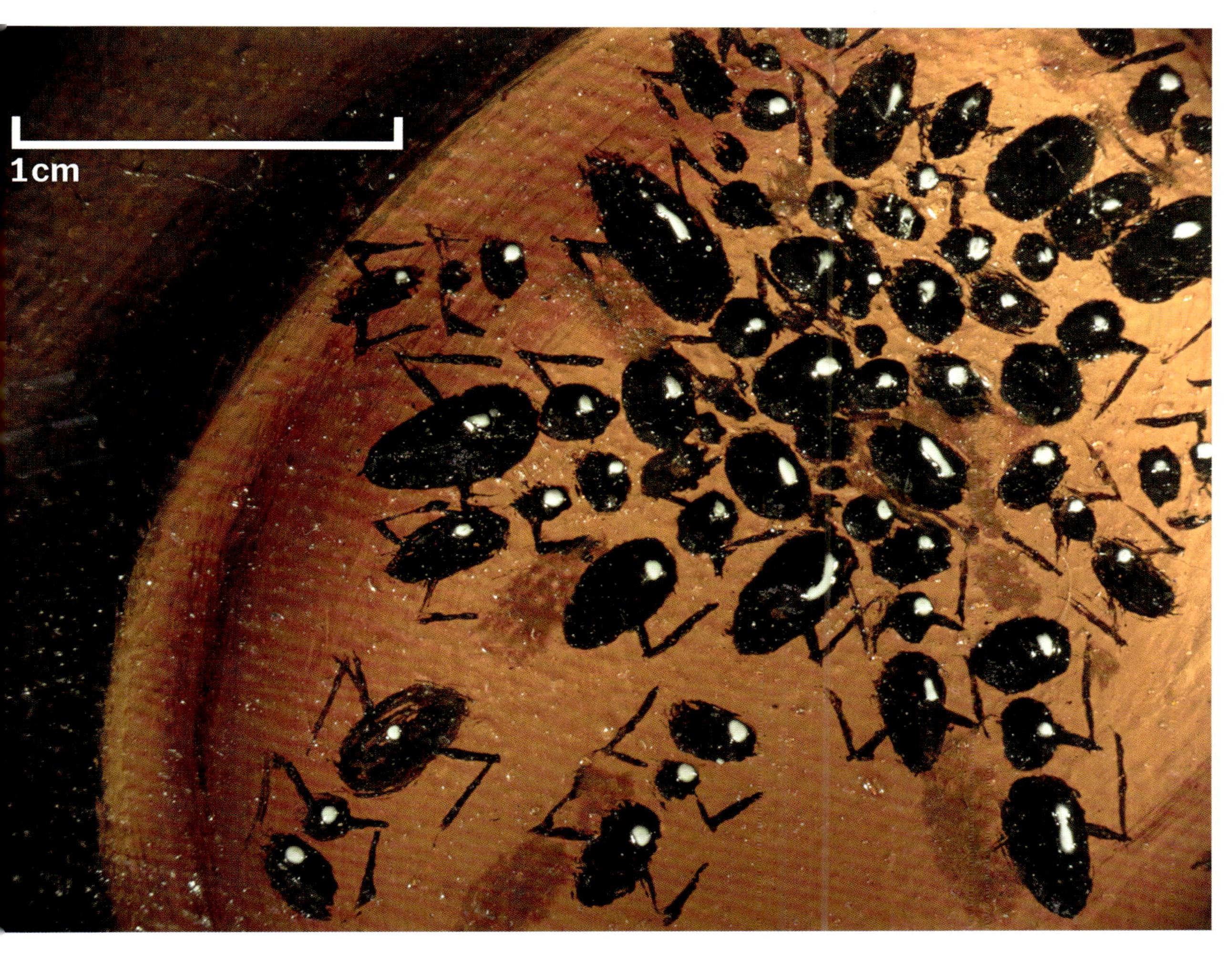

FIG. 20. *The Persistence of Memory*, detail photographed at 6x magnification

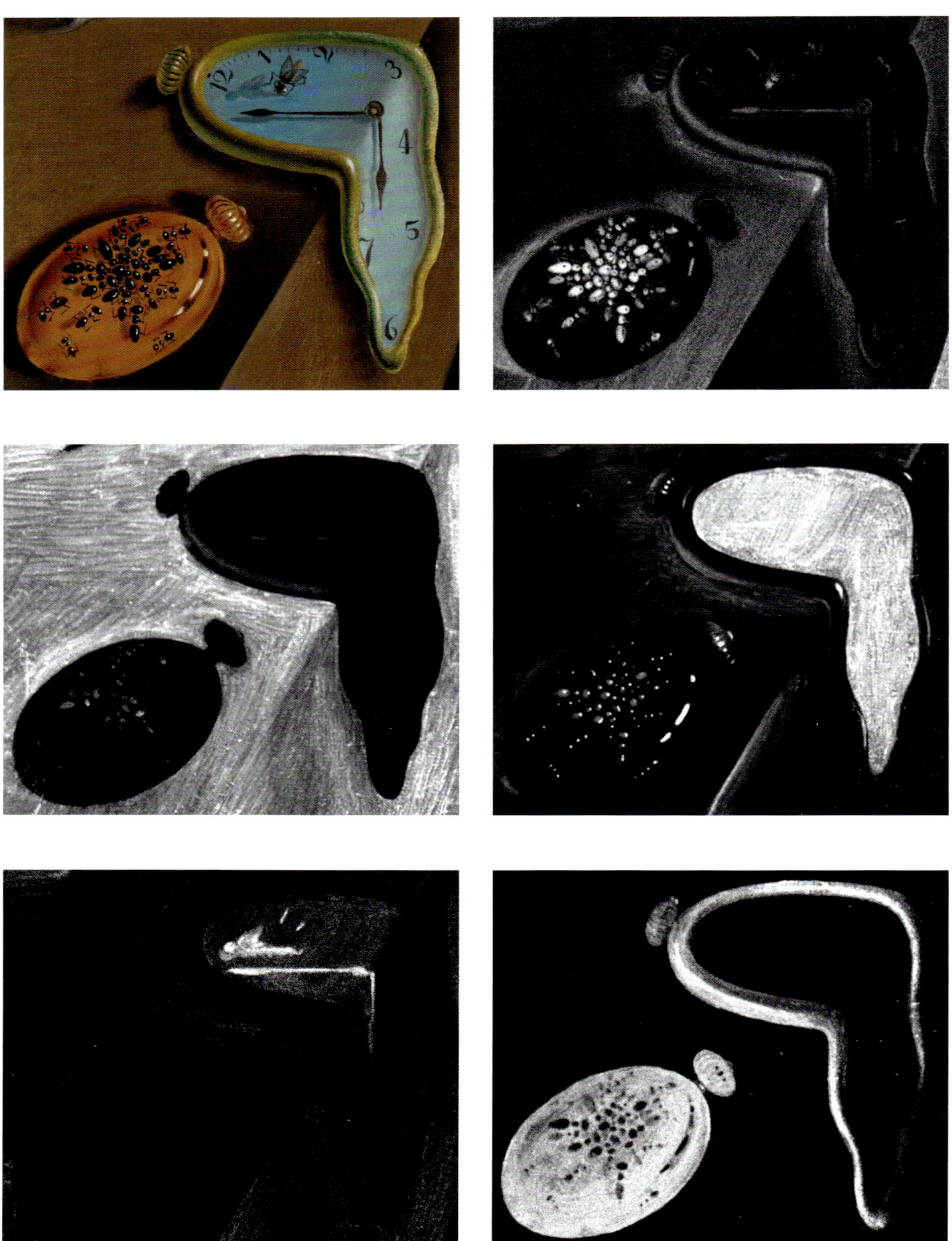

FIG. 21. X-ray fluorescence (XRF) maps identifying the location of specific pigments. Left to right, top to bottom: *The Persistence of Memory* (detail), bone black, earth brown, zinc white, cerulean blue, chrome yellow/orange

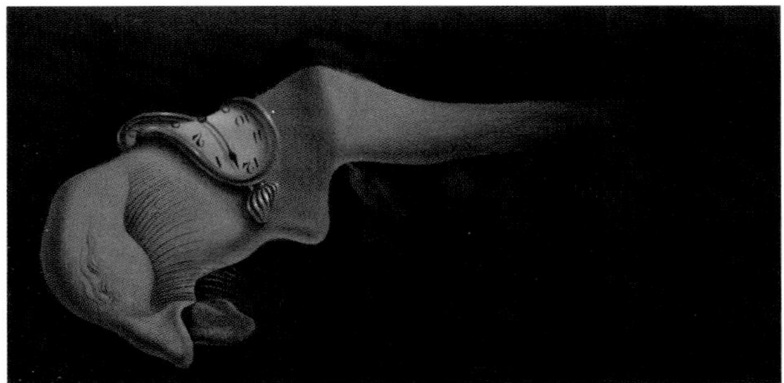
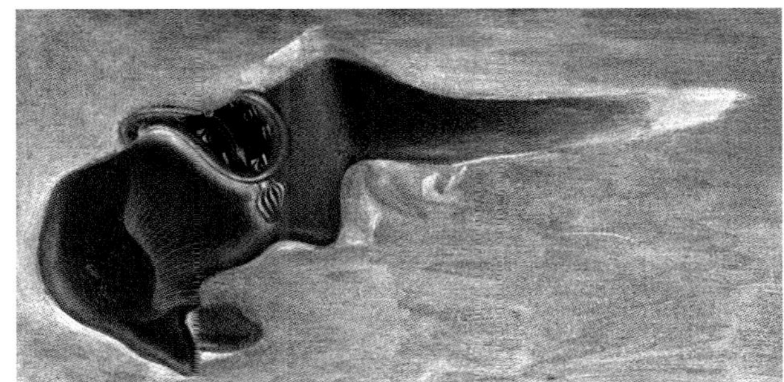
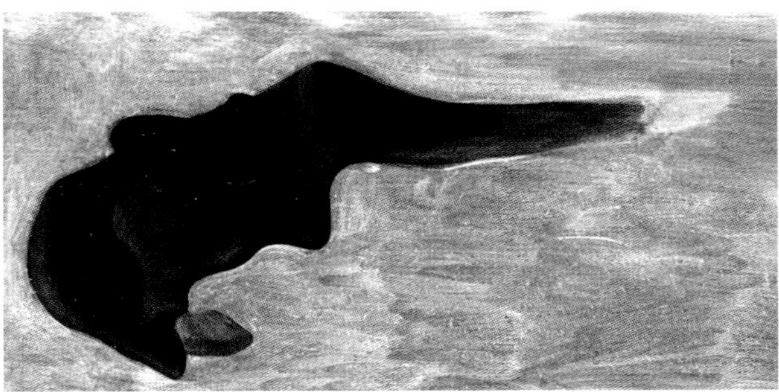
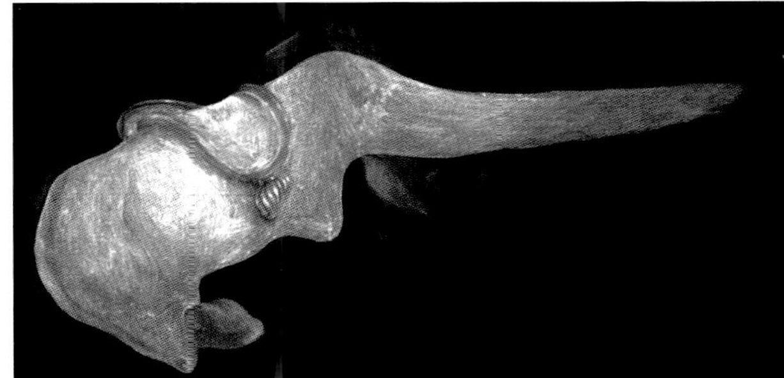

FIG. 22. X-ray fluorescence (XRF) maps identifying the location of specific pigments. Left to right, top to bottom: *The Persistence of Memory* (detail), bone black, earth brown, zinc white

bone-black and earth-brown paints that he used for the ground beneath it, which he filled in more rapidly, using larger brushes **[FIG. 22]**.

This entity, with what may or may not be a tongue emerging from its nose, goes unmentioned in Dalí's description of *The Persistence of Memory* in his autobiography, although in the immediately preceding passage he compares his own "tender nakedness" to that of a hermit crab, which adopts the hard shells of other sea creatures to protect its soft body.[21] An early full-face variant of the motif appears along the horizon line at left in *Futile Efforts*, where its resemblance to Dalí's own features is most evident; it appeared and reappeared in various guises, sizes, and states of disfiguration in numerous other works, most notably in *Face of the Great Masturbator*, where a terrifyingly large grasshopper clings to the place where its mouth should be. Unlike the watches, this beached creature resists easy description or identification; it is neither strictly animal nor human, male nor female—characteristics shared with certain of Miró's more abstract figures. It can also be compared with the nonconformist self-images created in the first half of the twentieth century by Claude Cahun (born Lucy Schwob) and her lifelong creative and romantic partner, Marcel Moore (born Suzanne Malherbe), who used the cut-and-paste techniques of collage to explore "the

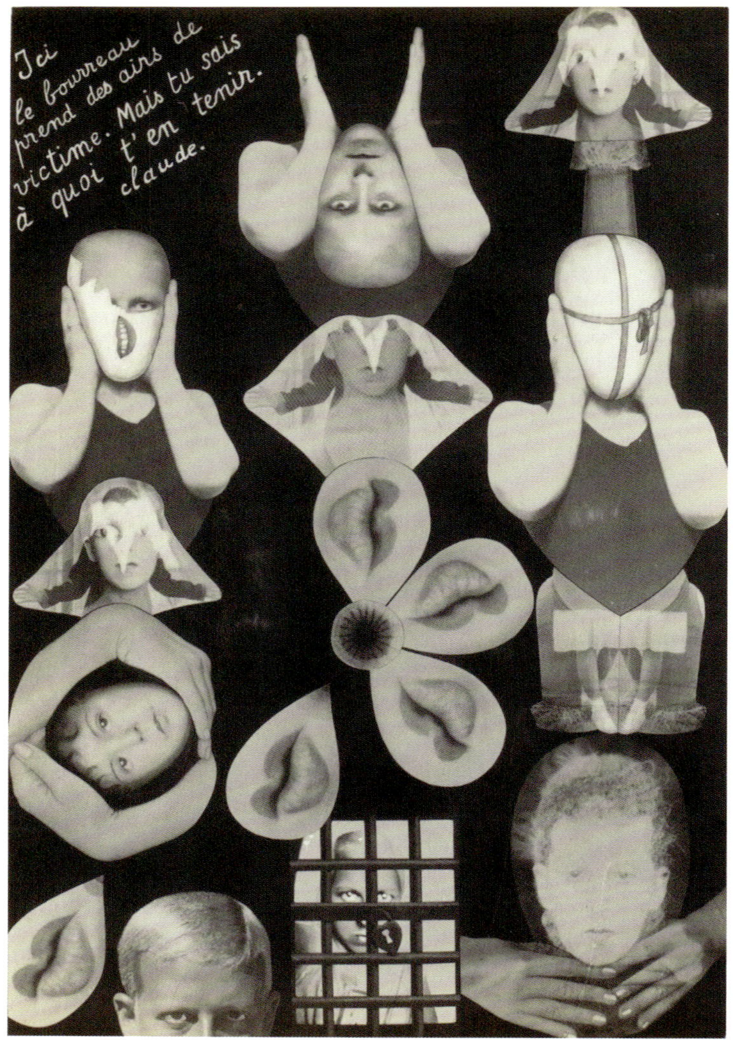

FIG. 23. Claude Cahun (French, 1894–1954). *M.R.M (Sex)*. c. 1929–30. Gelatin silver print, 6 × 4" (15.2 × 10.2 cm). THE MUSEUM OF MODERN ART, NEW YORK. GIFT OF HELEN KORNBLUM IN HONOR OF ROXANA MARCOCI

body's weirdnesses" and the "porous and blurred" divisions between genders **[FIG. 23]**.[22]

Dalí himself, in the exhibition catalogue for his June 1931 exhibition, implicitly associated his self-portrait and the watches that accompany it with his interest in "ornamental" or "modern-style" Art Nouveau objects and architecture. Only two of his works were illustrated in the catalogue—*The Persistence of Memory* and *Profanation of the Host* **[FIG. 24]**—accompanied by a statement

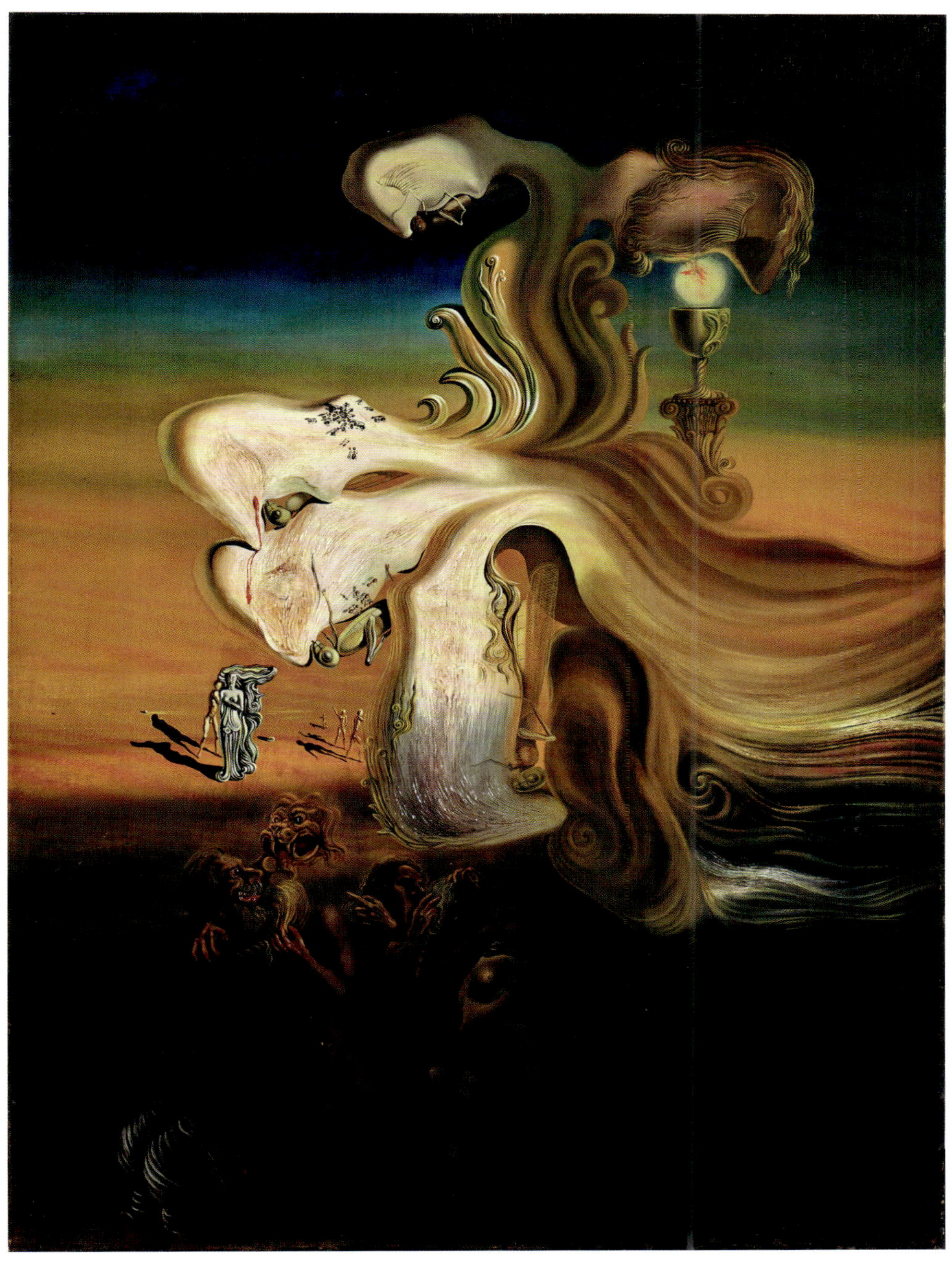

FIG. 24. Salvador Dalí (Spanish, 1904–1989). *Profanation of the Host*. c. 1930. Oil on canvas, 39 ⅜ × 28 ¾" (100 × 73 cm). THE DALÍ MUSEUM, ST. PETERSBURG, FLORIDA. GIFT OF A. REYNOLDS AND ELEANOR MORSE

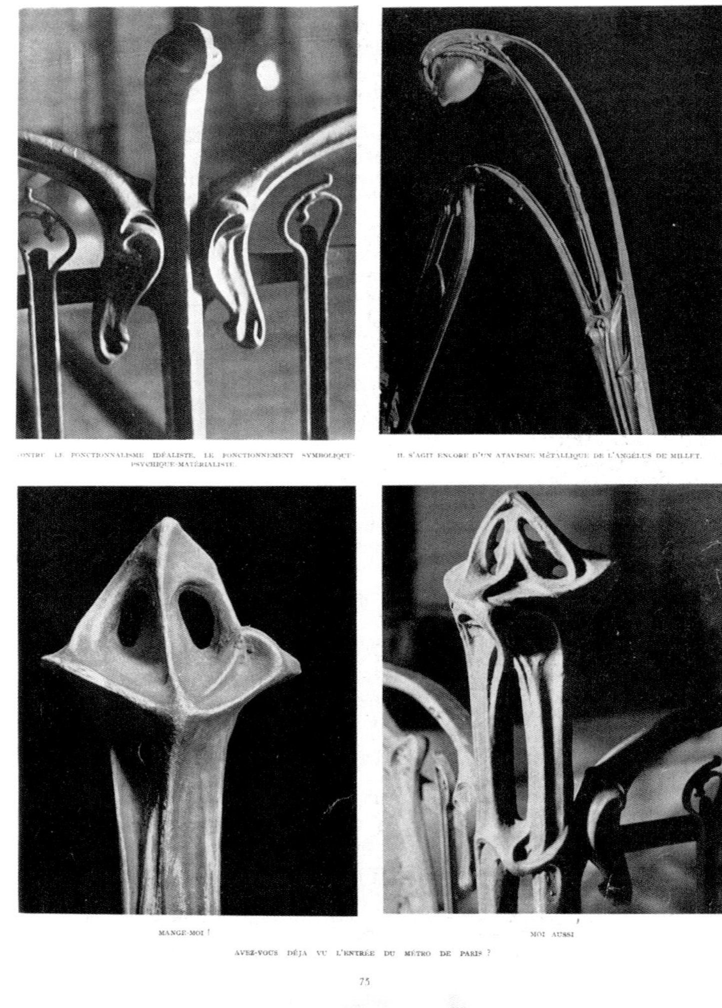
CONTRE LE FONCTIONNALISME IDÉALISTE, LE FONCTIONNEMENT SYMBOLIQUE-PSYCHIQUE-MATÉRIALISTE.

IL S'AGIT ENCORE D'UN ATAVISME MÉTALLIQUE DE L'ANGÉLUS DE MILLET.

MANGE-MOI !

MOI AUSSI

AVEZ-VOUS DÉJA VU L'ENTRÉE DU MÉTRO DE PARIS ?

73

FIG. 25. Brassaï (Gyula Halász) (French, born Transylvania. 1899–1984). Details of the Paris Metro (c. 1933), in Salvador Dalí, "De la beauté terrifiante et comestible, de l'architecture Modern' style," *Minotaure*, nos. 3–4 (December 1933), 73

in which Dalí declares that "ornamental objects of the 'modern-style' reveal to us in the most material way the persistence of dreams through reality."[23] This was achieved above all in "the wild and absolutely beautiful ornamentation of 'modern-style' metro entrances," specifically those by the Paris architect and designer Hector Guimard, which were "eaten away on all sides by the perpetual torment of corrosive reality" **[FIG. 25]**.[24] The gushing flourishes and sinuous curves of the towering monument at center in *Profanation of the Host*—from which no less than five Dalinian heads erupt, one with Christlike features—bear a family resemblance to Guimard's metro entrances. This structure and its appendages, like Dalí's malformed watches, engage with what the artist identifies in *The Secret Life of Salvador Dalí* as "the morphological esthetics of the soft and hard" and the "philosophic problems of the 'super-soft.'"[25] Each disrupts and disfigures the "reality of the external world" by eroding differences and distinctions between people and objects, metal and flesh, solid structures and those devoured by desire.[26] The goal: to reveal and make perceptible, via Dalí's deliberately cultivated "paranoiac" vision, hidden associations and relationships, like those between organic architectural ornamentation, quasi-human anatomies, and humble pocket watches.

At the close of Dalí's exhibition at Galerie Pierre Colle, *The Persistence of Memory* remained unsold. This allowed the young American dealer Julien Levy, who was preparing to open a new gallery on Madison Avenue in New York, to purchase it from Colle for $250 (about $5,000 today).[27] The painting spent some time stashed away in the eccentrically furnished Paris apartment of the writer and artist Mina Loy, who was working at the time as Levy's agent and representative.[28] Sometime prior to November 1931, *The Persistence of Memory* crossed the Atlantic for its North American debut. Levy lent it to the exhibition *Newer Super-Realism* at the Wadsworth Atheneum, in Hartford, Connecticut—the first exhibit on of Surrealist art in the United States, in which fifty works by various artists including de Chirico, Ernst, Miró, and Pablo Picasso were featured; of those fifty works, eight were by Dalí, including *The Persistence of Memory*. Although it seems to have been largely ignored by the Paris press, it became a media sensation almost from the first moment it arrived on the shores of the United States. It was reproduced and written about in local Hartford newspapers, and, in January 1932, when Levy staged his own Surrealism exhibition in New York City, it was featured prominently in the arts section of *The New York Times*.

Alfred H. Barr Jr., MoMA's founding director, may have seen *The Persistence of Memory* in Paris in 1931 and then again at Levy's show, to which he and his wife, Margaret Scolari Barr, lent an unattributed seventeenth-century landscape that, as the critic Edward Alden Jewell remarked, "if you turn it on end, becomes a portrait!"[29] *The Persistence of Memory* was featured again at Levy's gallery in Dalí's first solo exhibition there, held from November 21 to December 8, 1933. Subsequent correspondence between Barr and Levy indicates that Barr asked about the price of the work on at least two occasions, the first during or soon after the close of Dalí's exhibition, and then again at a party.[30] Between those two events, Levy upped his asking price from $300 to $400. On July 12, 1934, Barr wrote to Levy to tell him that he had found a donor who was willing to purchase *The Persistence of Memory* for the Museum for $350, an offer Levy accepted.[31] The donor was Mrs. Helen Resor, an advertising copywriter and executive who worked at the

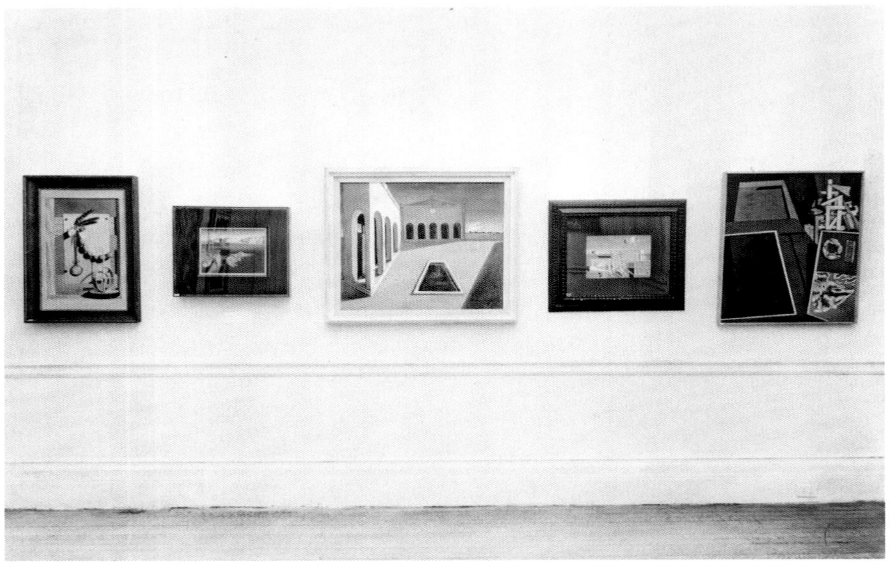

FIG. 26. Installation view of *Modern Works of Art: 5th Anniversary Exhibition,* The Museum of Modern Art, New York, November 19, 1934–January 20, 1935. THE MUSEUM OF MODERN ART ARCHIVES, NEW YORK

legendary agency J. Walter Thompson. In retrospect, it seems oddly fitting that the purchase was funded by someone who worked in advertising: *The Persistence of Memory* very quickly became a recognizable logo or emblem of what we would now call Dalí's signature Surrealist brand. In Barr's letters to various trustees, for example, when soliciting support for this acquisition, he frequently referred to *The Persistence of Memory*'s "already famous" character.[32] On November 20, 1934, the new acquisition went on view at the Museum for the first time, in *Modern Works of Art: 5th Anniversary Exhibition* **[FIG. 26]**. For reasons that remain unknown, Resor asked that the credit line for the work read "Given anonymously." But her identity was an open secret and was mentioned in an article in *The New York Times* about the painting's first appearance at the Museum.[33] Since then it has featured in innumerable collection displays and exhibitions at MoMA and elsewhere, remaining perpetually on public view.

Dalí also tended to the fame of *The Persistence of Memory*, in part by continuing to produce variants of it.[34] In 1939, he recreated it on a vast scale as a mural for his *Dream of Venus* pavilion at the New York World's Fair **[FIG. 27]**.[35] In 1942, he chose it as the cover image for *The Secret Life of Salvador Dalí* **[FIG. 28]**. In 1952–54, he created *The Disintegration of the Persistence of Memory* **[FIG. 29]**, an updated version nearly identical in size but newly populated by tiny rectangular blocks and rhinoceros horns that suggest atomic particles floating in space, in keeping with his post–World War II interest in theories of nuclear physics. Also

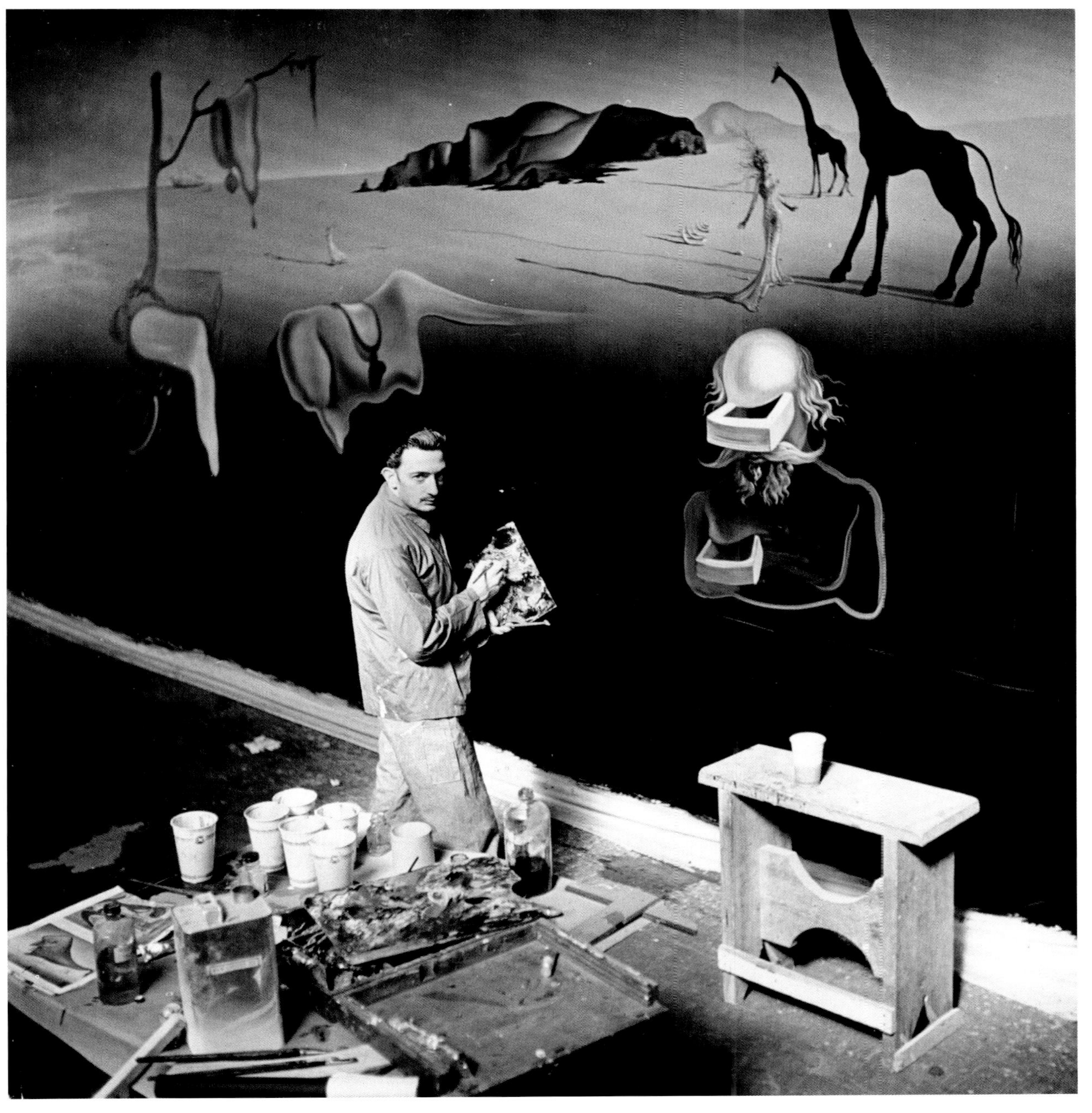

FIG. 27. Eric Schaal (German, 1905–1994). Salvador Dalí in *The Dream of Venus* pavilion. 1939. Gelatin silver print, 8 ½ × 8 ⅛" (21.5 × 20.7 cm). FUNDACIÓ GALA-SALVADOR DALÍ, FIGUERES

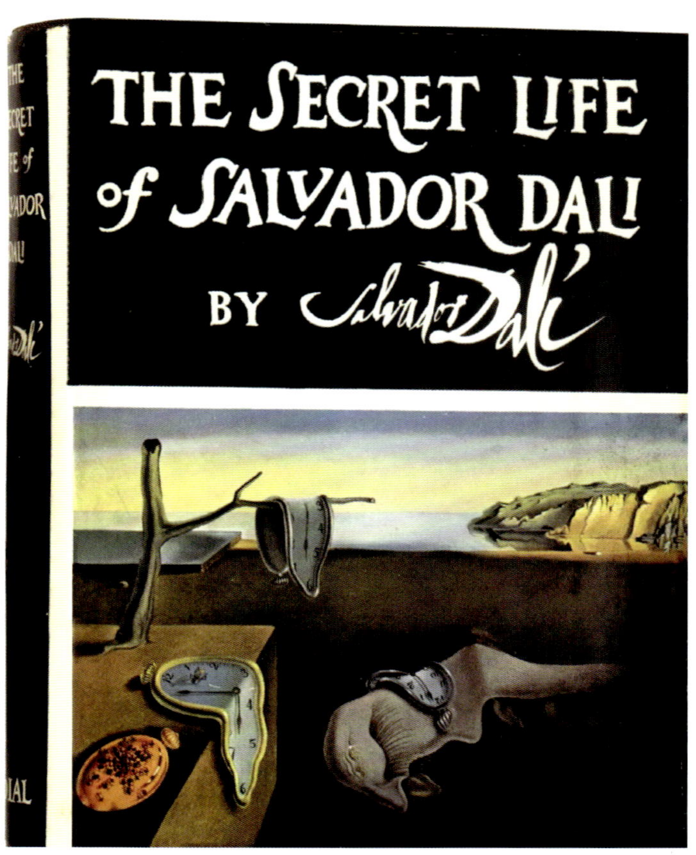

FIG. 28. Cover of Salvador Dalí, *The Secret Life of Salvador Dalí* (New York: Dial, 1942)

during the 1950s, he collaborated with the photographer Philippe Halsman to create a hilarious photomontage version of *The Persistence of Memory* with his own face inserted in place of one of the watches; it was first published in the small book *Dalí's Mustache: A Photographic Interview*, accompanied by the caption "Surrealism is myself" **[FIG. 30]**.[36] And in 1975, he authorized the production of a tapestry nearly five feet high, in an edition of five hundred, in which *The Persistence of Memory* appears surrounded by an elaborate gold frame and four crowns **[FIG. 31]**. The tapestry is a reminder of Dalí's commercial exploitation of his own work, for which he was often criticized, the first time by Breton, who, in 1940, in a fit of pique—fed up with Dalí's savvy marketing and his offensive alignment with the Fascist Spanish dictator Francisco Franco—nicknamed him "Avida Dollars."

Given the oversized reputation of both Dalí and *The Persistence of Memory*, it may be surprising for those who have not seen it in person to discover just how

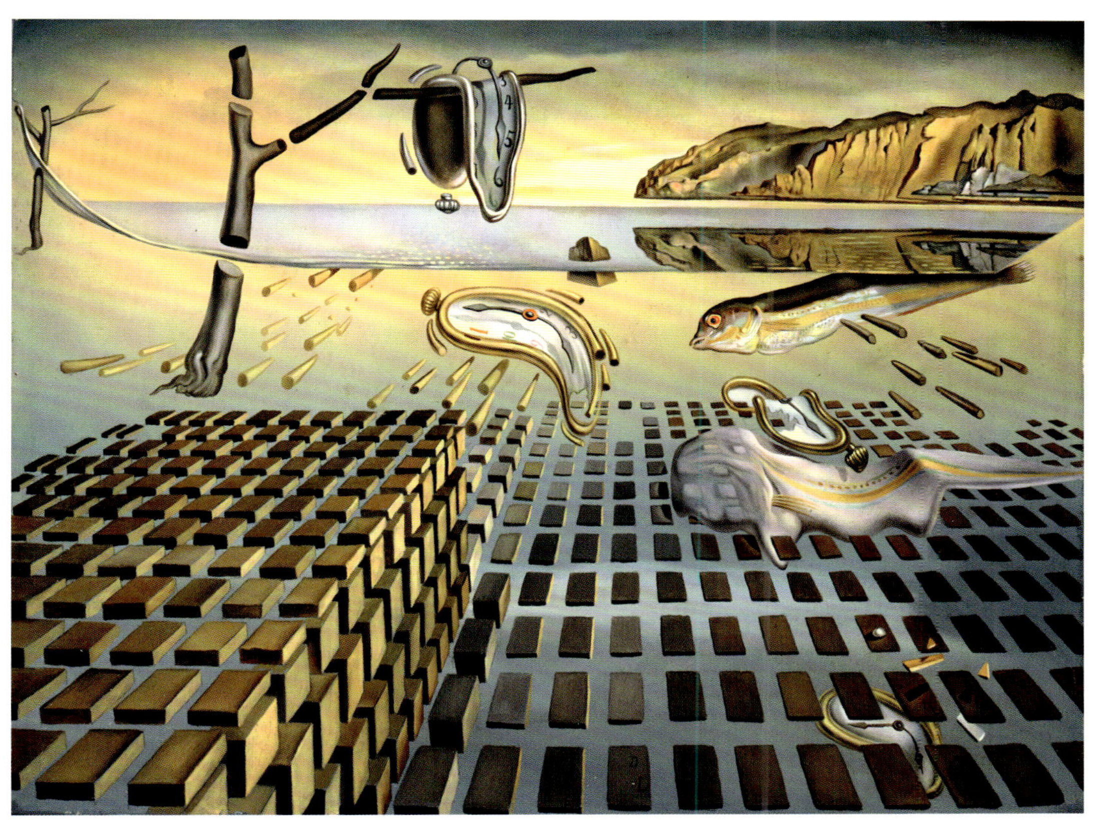

FIG. 29. Salvador Dalí (Spanish, 1904–1989). *The Disintegration of the Persistence of Memory.* 1952–54. Oil on canvas, 10 × 13" (25.4 × 33 cm). THE DALÍ MUSEUM, ST. PETERSBURG, FLORIDA. GIFT OF A. REYNOLDS AND ELEANOR MORSE

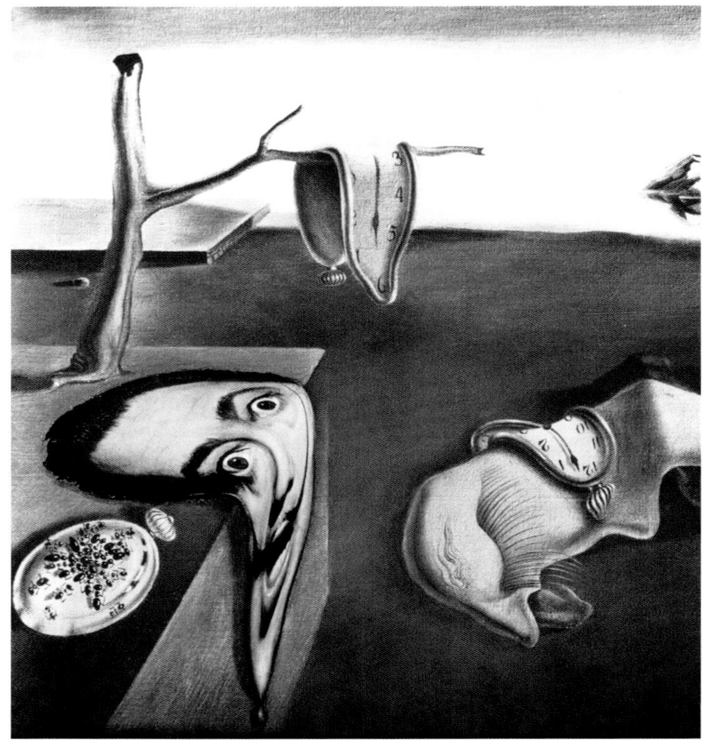

FIG. 30. Philippe Halsman (American, born Latvia. 1906–1979). *Surrealism Is Myself.* 1954. Gelatin silver print. PHILIPPE HALSMAN ARCHIVE/MAGNUM PHOTOS

small it is. The comedian Steve Martin fondly recalls an early visit to "glorious Manhattan," where "saucer-eyed, we hustled over to the Museum of Modern Art, where we saw, among the Cézannes and Matisses, Dalí's famous painting of melting clocks, the shockingly tiny *The Persistence of Memory*."[37] Today, this "shockingly tiny" painting is displayed on its own wall in the Museum's fifth-floor collection galleries, among works by Dalí's contemporaries whose larger size and bold legibility underscore *The Persistence of Memory*'s delicately painted miniature qualities and its disproportionately powerful allure **[FIG. 32]**. Working within the tradition of the tiny, Dalí created a picture that is both an icon—in the literal sense of a small devotional painting—and iconic, possessed of an aura that exceeds its material bounds. It is, moreover, a work that begs to be examined closely, to be marveled at, and to have time taken with. Time, of course, is something we each experience, consciously or not, every day, minute, and second, in individual ways. To capture and make visible its inexorable melt, its elastic capacity, its familiar yet repulsive qualities in a way that "no one can forget once [they've] seen it" is no small thing.

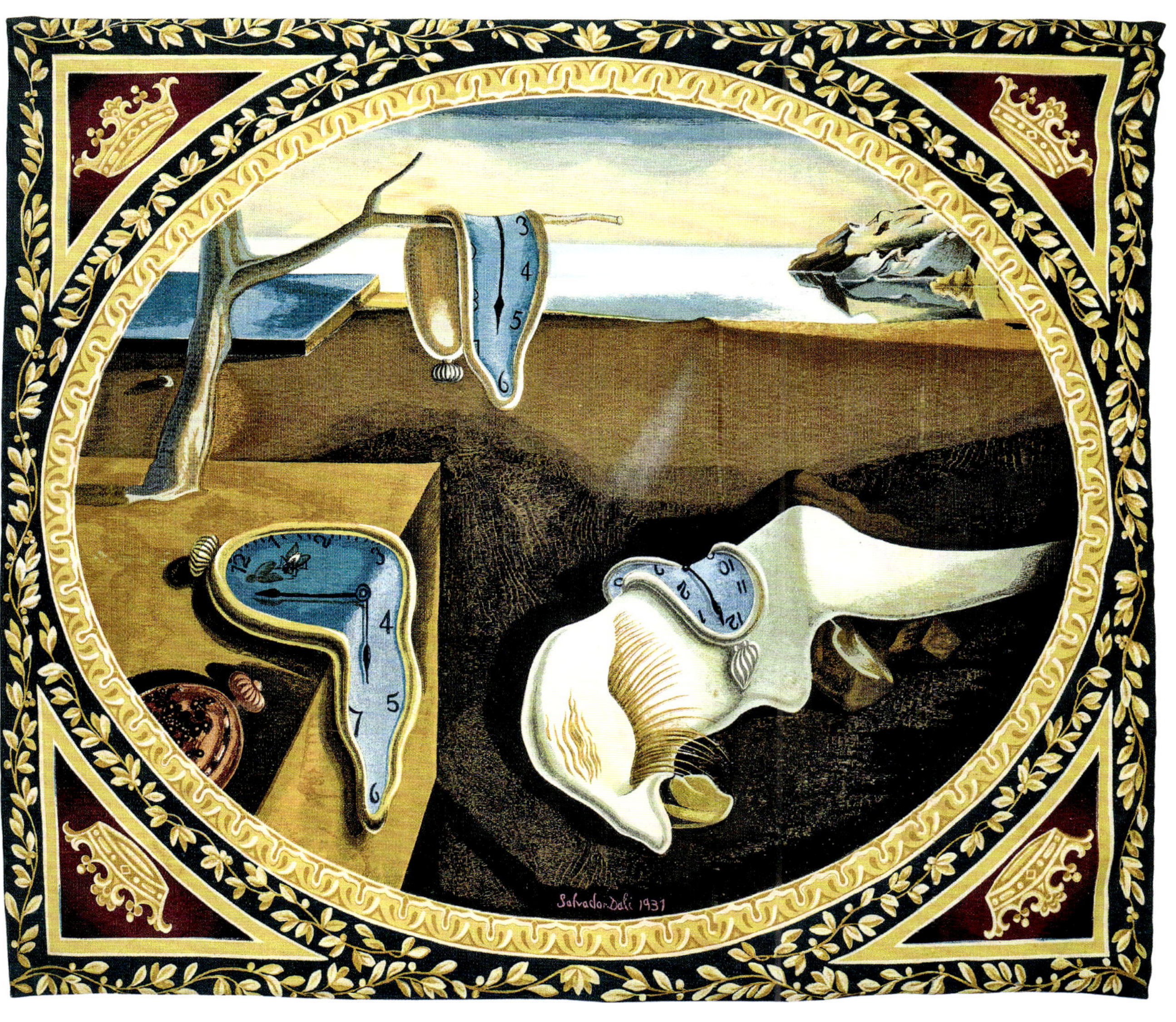

FIG. 31. After Salvador Dalí. *The Persistence of Memory Tapestry*. *1975*. Wool tapestry, 55 × 66″ (139.7 × 167.6 cm). Edition: 48/500. PRIVATE COLLECTION

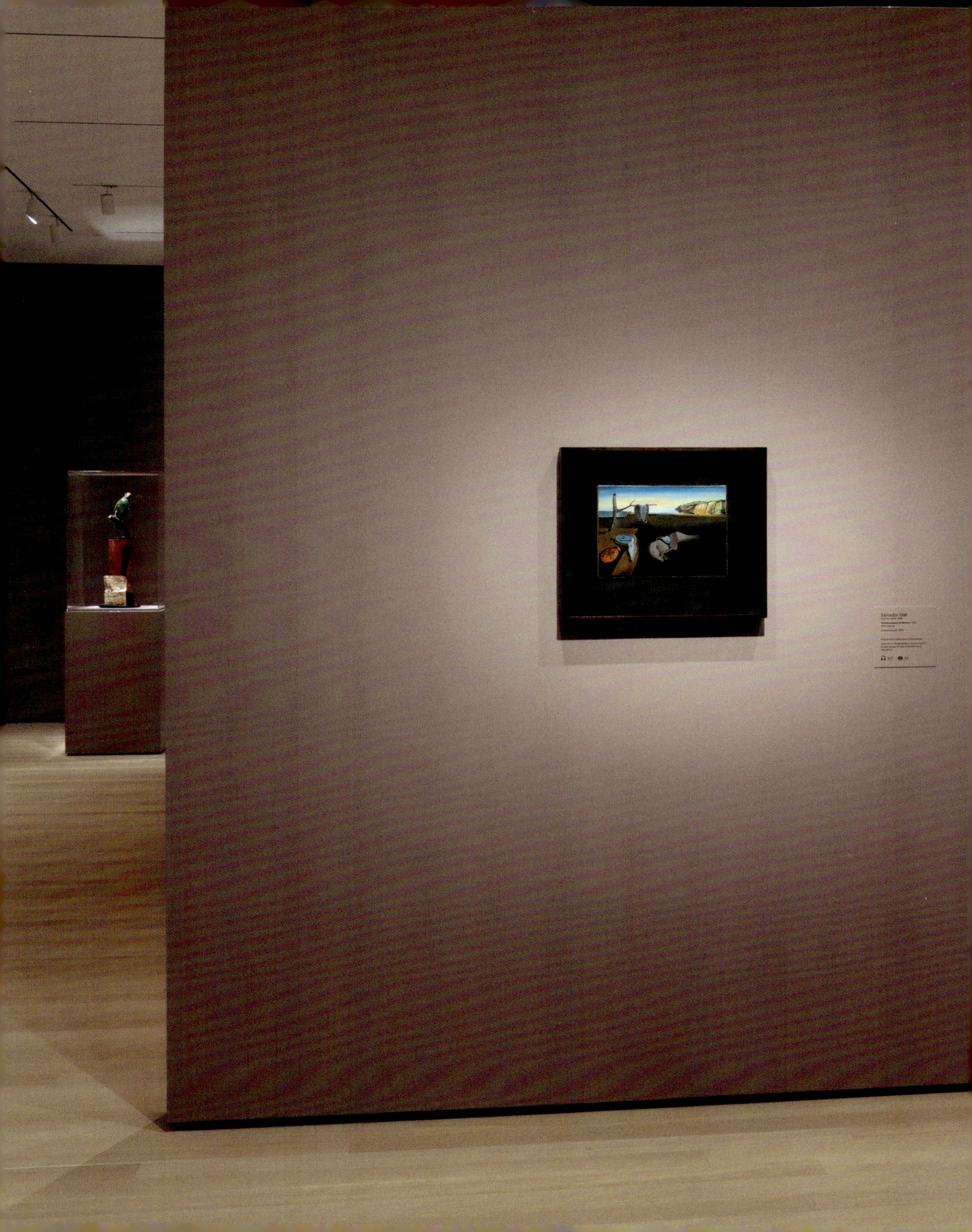
Salvador Dalí

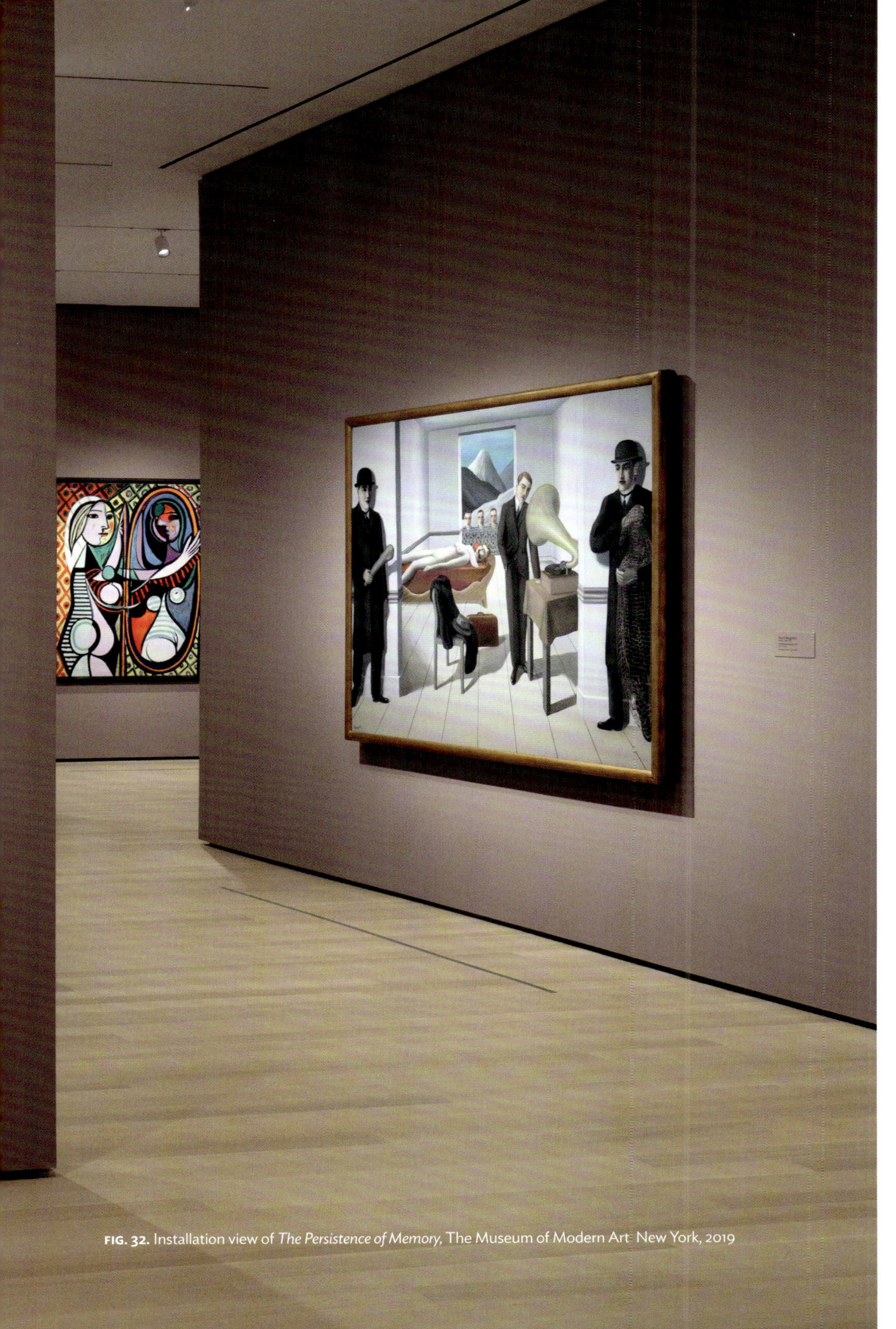

FIG. 32. Installation view of *The Persistence of Memory*, The Museum of Modern Art, New York, 2019

NOTES

For their invaluable insights and essential research support, I am deeply grateful to Alexandra Morrison, Department of Painting and Sculpture, and Anny Aviram, Michael Duffy, Abed Haddad, Emily Landry, Adam Neese, and Magdalena Solano, Department of Conservation, The Museum of Modern Art, New York. For general biographical information, I have relied on two indispensable publications: Dawn Ades, *Dalí*, World of Art, 3rd ed. (London: Thames and Hudson, 2022); and Ades and Michael Taylor with Montserrat Aguer, eds., *Dalí* (New York: Rizzoli, 2004).

1. Salvador Dalí, *The Secret Life of Salvador Dalí*, trans. Haakon M. Chevalier (New York: Dial, 1942), 317.
2. Dalí, MoMA Object Questionnaire, *The Persistence of Memory* (1931), undated [c. 1945]. Department of Painting and Sculpture, Museum Collection Files, The Museum of Modern Art, New York.
3. Dalí, *Secret Life of Salvador Dalí*, 317.
4. Dalí, *Secret Life of Salvador Dalí*, 317.
5. X-ray fluorescence spectroscopy (XRF) is a technique used by conservation scientists to analyze and identify elements that make up inorganic pigments. Scanning XRF generates distribution "maps" that illustrate the occurrence of each element across the composition.
6. André Breton, "The Dalí 'Case,'" 1936, in *Surrealism and Painting*, trans. Simon Watson Taylor (Boston: MFA Publications, 2002), 195, quoted in Ades, *Dalí*, 6.
7. For Dalí's first use of the full term "paranoiac critical," around 1933, see Ades, *Dalí*, 133.
8. Dalí, "The Rotting Donkey," in *The Collected Writings of Salvador Dalí*, ed. and trans. Haim Finkelstein, 2nd ed. (St. Petersburg, FL: Dalí Museum, 2017), 223. Originally published as "L'Âne pourri," in *La Femme visible* (Paris: Éditions surréalistes, 1930), 11–20; and in *Le Surréalisme au service de la révolution*, no. 1 (July 1930): 9–12.
9. Ades, *Dalí*, 27–28.
10. On possible connections between Dalí's father's pocket watch and the melting watches in *The Persistence of Memory*, see Elliott King, "Le Temps dalínien fait mouche: Réflexions sur les 'montres molles,'" in *Salvador Dalí à la croisée des savoirs*, ed. Astrid Ruffa, Philippe Kaenel, and Danielle Chaperon (Paris: Éditions Desjonquères, 2007), 41–43.
11. Salvador Dalí Cusí, letter to Joan Miró, May 17, 1929. Arxiu Successió Joan Miró, Palma de Mallorca.
12. Miró, letter to Dalí, March 13, 1929, trans. in *Salvador Dalí: The Early Years*, ed. Michael Raeburn (London: South Bank Centre, 1994), 40.
13. Dalí, letter to Federico García Lorca, March 1926, quoted in Ades, *Dalí*, 51; and "Sant Sebastià," *L'Amic de les Arts* 2, no. 16 (July 31, 1927): 52–54, in *The Collected Writings of Salvador Dalí*, 2.
14. Miró, letter to Sebastià Gasch, April 9, 1929, in *Epistolari Català Joan Miró, 1911–1945*, ed. Joan M. Minguet, Teresa Montaner, and Joan Santanach (Barcelona: Editorial Barcino/Fundació Joan Miró, 2009), 390, trans. by Cristina Portell and Mary Ann Newman.
15. The other pre-1929 painting included in the exhibition was *Apparatus and Hand* (1927).
16. Ades, *Dalí*, 103.
17. Dalí, *Secret Life of Salvador Dalí*, 248n1. Éluard and Gala divorced on July 15, 1932; she and Dalí married on January 30, 1934.
18. Dalí, *Secret Life of Salvador Dalí*, 317.
19. On the significance of this scale in Dalí's work and its relation to the tradition of small-format painting, see Roger Rothman, *Tiny Surrealism: Salvador Dalí and the Aesthetics of the Small* (Lincoln: University of Nebraska Press, 2012); and Mark A. Roglán and Shelley DeMaria, eds. *Dalí: Poetics of the Small, 1929–36* (Dallas: Meadows Museum, SMU, 2018).
20. Dalí, "Rotting Donkey," 223.
21. Dalí, *Secret Life of Salvador Dalí*, 317.
22. My framing of Cahun and Moore's project draws upon Kolleen Ku, "Claude Cahun (Lucy Schwob), *M.R.M. (Sex)* (c. 1929–30)," Museum Research Consortium Study Session, The Museum of Modern Art, New York, May 2, 2024. The quotations come from Ariella Budick, "MoMA Uses Abstraction to Politicise the Past in *Vital Signs*," *Financial Times*, December 11, 2024.
23. Dalí, ". . . Surtout, l'art ornemental . . . ", in *Dalí* (Paris: Galerie Pierre Colle, 1931), trans. in Ades, *Dalí*, 191.
24. Dalí, "Surtout," additional trans. by Alexandra Morrison.
25. Dalí, *Secret Life of Salvador Dalí*, 304, 317.
26. Dalí, "Rotting Donkey," 223.
27. Julien Levy, *Memoir of an Art Gallery* (New York: G. P. Putnam's Sons, 1977), 71. Levy's financial ledger indicates he paid only $165 for *The Persistence of*

Memory, including $12 for framing, $21 for export, and $4 for customs duties. Financial ledger, circa 1929–35. Julien Levy Gallery Records, Philadelphia Museum of Art, Library and Archives. Many thanks to Rona Razon for her kind assistance.

28. Ingrid Schaffner and Lisa Jacobs, eds., *Julien Levy: Portrait of an Art Gallery* (Cambridge, MA: MIT Press, 1998), 67, 69.

29. Edward Alden Jewell, "A Bewildering Exhibition," *New York Times*, January 13, 1932, 2. Barr was in Paris in the summer of 1931, where he saw Dalí and visited Pierre Colle's gallery. Margaret Scolari Barr, "Our Campaigns: 1930–1944," in "Our Campaigns," ed. Hilton Kramer, special issue, *New Criterion*, Summer 1987, 26–27.

30. Alfred H. Barr Jr., letter to Levy, June 28, 1934. Alfred H. Barr, Jr. Papers, mf 2165:441. The Museum of Modern Art Archives, New York.

31. Barr, letter to Levy, July 12, 1934. Department of Painting and Sculpture, Museum Collection Files, The Museum of Modern Art, New York.

32. Barr, letters to A. Conger Goodyear, July 12, 1934; Samuel Lewisohn, July 12, 1934; and Edward M. M. Warburg, July 12, 1934. Department of Painting and Sculpture, Museum Collection Files, The Museum of Modern Art, New York.

33. Jewell, "Show at Museum Marks Fifth Year," *New York Times*, November 20, 1934, 19.

34. He also referred to it frequently in his writing over the years, the first time memorably describing his "famous flabby watches" as "nothing else than the tender, extravagant and solitary paranoiac-critical Camembert of time and space." Dalí, *Conquest of the Irrational*, trans. David Gascoyne (New York: Julien Levy, 1935), 25.

35. Painted in oil on canvas on four panels of Masonite, Dalí's portable mural *The Dream of Venus* (1939) is owned by Hiroshima Prefectural Art Museum, Japan.

36. Dalí and Philippe Halsman, *Dalí's Mustache: A Photographic Interview*, 2nd ed. (Paris: Flammarion, 1994), 67, 122. The book is dedicated "to Gala, who is the guardian angel of my mustache also."

37. Steve Martin, *Born Standing Up: A Comic's Life* (New York: Scribner, 2007), 79. Thanks to Lewis Kachur for bringing this reference to my attention.

FOR FURTHER READING

Ades, Dawn. *Dalí*. World of Art. 3rd ed. London: Thames and Hudson, 2022.

Ades, Dawn, and Michael Taylor with Montserrat Aguer, eds. *Dalí*. Exh. cat. New York: Rizzoli, 2004.

Dalí, Salvador. *The Secret Life of Salvador Dalí*. Translated by Haakon M. Chevalier. New York: Dial, 1942.

Dalí, Salvador. *The Collected Writings of Salvador Dalí*. 2nd ed. Edited and translated by Haim Finkelstein. St. Petersburg, FL: Dalí Museum, 2017.

Raeburn, Michael, ed. *Salvador Dalí: The Early Years*. Exh. cat. London: South Bank Centre, 1994.

Roglán, Mark A., and Shelly DeMaria, eds. *Dalí: Poetics of the Small, 1929–36*. Exh. cat. Dallas: Meadows Museum, Southern Methodist University, 2018.

Rothman, Roger. *Tiny Surrealism: Salvador Dalí and the Aesthetics of the Small*. Lincoln: University of Nebraska Press, 2012.

Soby, James Thrall. *Salvador Dalí: Paintings, Drawings, Prints*. Exh. cat. New York: The Museum of Modern Art, 1941.

Leadership support for this publication is provided by the Kate W. Cassidy Foundation.

Produced by the Department of Publications
The Museum of Modern Art, New York

Leadership support for this publication is provided by the Kate W. Cassidy Foundation.

Michelle Kuo, Chief Curator at Large and Publisher
Curtis R. Scott, Associate Publisher
Hannah Kim, Business and Marketing Director
Joseph Mohan, Production Director
Anna Barnet, Managing Editor

Edited by Emily Hall
Series designed by Miko McGinty and Rita Jules
Layout by Amanda Washburn with Julia Brukx
Production by Matthew Pimm
Image rights and acquisition by Anne Levine
Proofread by Virginia Gresham
Printed and bound by Offset Yapımevi, Istanbul

This book is typeset in Ideal Sans.
The paper is 150 gsm Magno Satin.

Published by The Museum of Modern Art
11 West 53 Street
New York, NY 10019-5497
www.moma.org

ISBN: 978-1-63345-175-9

Distributed in the United States and Canada by
ARTBOOK | D.A.P.
75 Broad Street, Suite 630
New York, NY 10004
www.artbook.com

Distributed outside the United States and Canada by
Thames & Hudson
6-24 Britannia Street
London WC1X 9JD
www.thamesandhudson.com

Printed and bound in Turkey

Photograph Credits
In reproducing the images contained in this publication, the Museum obtained the permission of the rights holders whenever possible. If the Museum could not locate the rights holders, notwithstanding good-faith efforts, it requests that any contact information concerning such rights holders be forwarded so that they may be contacted for future editions.

All works by Salvador Dalí: © 2025 Salvador Dalí, Fundació Gala-Salvador Dalí, Artists Rights Society

The Art Institute of Chicago / Art Resource, New York: p. 22. © 2025 Artists Rights Society (ARS), New York / ADAGP, Paris: p. 19. © 2025 Artists Rights Society (ARS), New York / SIAE, Rome: p. 18. Bibliothèque nationale de France: p. 32. © Estate Brassaï - RMN Grand Palais: p. 32. The Dalí Museum, St. Petersburg, Florida: p. 37. © DeA Picture Library / Art Resource, New York: p. 16. Fundació Gala-Salvador Dalí, Figueres: p. 9. © Philippe Halsman / Magnum Photos: p. 38. © 2025 C. Herscovici / Artists Rights Society (ARS), New York: pp. 22, 40–41. © Man Ray 2015 Trust / Artists Rights Society (ARS), NY / ADAGP, Paris 2025: p. 4. Image copyright © The Metropolitan Museum of Art. Image source: Art Resource, New York: p. 15. © Successió Miró / Artists Rights Society (ARS), New York / ADAGP, Paris 2025: pp. 20, 40–41. Museo Nacional Centro de Arte Reina Sofía, Madrid: pp. 11, 12. Image copyright © Museo Nacional del Prado / Art Resource, New York: p. 17. The Museum of Modern Art, New York, The David Booth Conservation Department, photograph by Abed Haddad: pp. 7, 28, 29; photograph by Emily Landry and Magdalena Solano: pp. 24, 26, 27. Digital Image © 2025 The Museum of Modern Art, New York, Film Stills Archive: p. 10. Digital Image © 2025 The Museum of Modern Art, New York, Imaging and Visual Resources Department, photograph by Jonathan David Almeida: p. 23; photograph by Jonathan Muzikar: cover, pp. 2–3, 4, 14, 18, 19, 30, 40–41. The Museum of Modern Art Archives, New York, photography by Soichi Sunami: p. 34. © 2025 Estate of Pablo Picasso / Artists Rights Society (ARS), New York: pp. 40–1. Pinakothek der Moderne, Munich - ARTOTHEK: p. 13. Eric Schaal © Fundació Gala-Salvador Dalí, Figueres, 2025 p. 35. Courtesy of Shapiro Auctions, New York: p. 39. Photograph © Joseph Siciliano USA, 2016: p. 31. © Estate of Yves Tanguy / Artists Rights Society (ARS), New York: p. 21.

TRUSTEES OF THE MUSEUM OF MODERN ART